The talkSPORT QUIZ BOOK

The talkSPORT QUIZ BOOK

Compiled by
NATHAN JOYCE

HarperCollins*Publishers*

HarperCollins*Publishers*
1 London Bridge Street
London SE1 9GF

www.harpercollins.co.uk

HarperCollins*Publishers*
1st Floor, Watermarque Building, Ringsend Road
Dublin 4, Ireland

First published by HarperCollins*Publishers* 2021

1 3 5 7 9 10 8 6 4 2

A catalogue record of this book is
available from the British Library

ISBN 978-0-00-849061-4

Printed and bound in the UK using 100%
renewable electricity at CPI Group (UK) Ltd

MIX
Paper from
responsible sources
FSC™ C007454

This book is produced from independently certified FSC™ paper
to ensure responsible forest management.

For more information visit: www.harpercollins.co.uk/green

CONTENTS

INTRODUCTION 1

FOOTBALL
EASY 5
MEDIUM 17
HARD 40

BOXING
EASY 71
MEDIUM 74
HARD 77

CRICKET
EASY 85
MEDIUM 91
HARD 102

DARTS
EASY 115
MEDIUM 117
HARD 119

F1
EASY 125
MEDIUM 128
HARD 132

GOLF
EASY 137
MEDIUM 140
HARD 143

HORSE RACING
EASY 149
MEDIUM 151
HARD 153

RUGBY LEAGUE
EASY 159
MEDIUM 161
HARD 163

RUGBY UNION
EASY 167
MEDIUM 172
HARD 176

TENNIS
EASY 183
MEDIUM 185
HARD 188

US SPORTS
NFL 193
NBA 194
MLB 195

ANSWERS 197

INTRODUCTION

I've been up in the attic digging out my old annuals and programmes to help create the first ever *talkSPORT Quiz Book*, featuring all the sports we love and cover live on radio and on our website. It's no secret that we love the beautiful game. But we're big on boxing, cricket, darts, F1, golf, horse racing, rugby league, rugby union, tennis and US sports too.

Inside you'll find more than 2,500 sports quiz questions and there's something for everyone.

Each sport includes three levels of difficulty, from easy, that anyone from young to old can have a go at, to the trickier medium section – think an away game at the Britannia on a wet, windy Wednesday evening in winter. And for those of you who like to dig out an obscure fact for a pub quiz, like which club were the Chuckle Brothers made honorary presidents of in 2007 or was the Rugby League World Cup trophy ever nicked from the Midland Hotel in Bradford in 1970, there's the hard section. (Adrian Durham would have known that one. Do alright in this and you've a right to be smug and call yourself a talkSPORT listener.)

In the super-size football section, you'll be called upon, among other things, to remember moments of commentary gold, deadline day deals (for God's sake, don't call my pal 'Arry Redknapp a wheeler dealer if you know what's good for you), chants from the terraces and throwback team sponsors. I bet Salvador Dalí couldn't have predicted that his Chupa Chups logo would end up on Sheffield Wednesday's kit in 2000!

And then there are the gaffes and wonderful moments, like Vinnie Jones trying to rip off Gazza's crown jewels at Plough Lane in 1988 and Freddie Flintoff warning Tino Best to 'mind the windows'.

There are questions on Jim White's transfer windows, Darren Bent's goal off a big red object (remember?) and even my co-host Ally McCoist's beloved Rangers feature.

Right, I'll wrap this up now before I give away too many of the answers. So, enjoy! It's been a lot of fun putting it together.

Alan Brazil

FOOTBALL

(ANSWERS PAGE 199)

talkSPORT has been broadcasting live Premier League, EFL, World Cup, Euros, Champions League and FA Cup matches since as far back as we can remember. In the football section, as throughout the book, we've got questions for all ages and expertise. So get your boots on and let's get going!

FOOTBALL (EASY)

WHERE IN THE WORLD?

1. Lazio, Sampdoria and Udinese compete in which country's top league?
   A: Sweden **B:** Italy **C:** Germany

2. The J1 League is the top league in which country?
   A: Japan **B:** Jordan **C:** Jamaica

3. Bayer Leverkusen and Borussia Dortmund play in which country's top league?
   A: Poland **B:** Netherlands **C:** Germany

4. Corinthians and Flamengo are two of which country's most famous teams?
   A: Iceland **B:** Brazil **C:** Russia

5. Feyenoord and PSV Eindhoven play in which country's top league?
   A: Belgium **B:** Netherlands **C:** France

6. The K League 1 is the top league in which country?
   A: Kenya **B:** Kuwait **C:** South Korea

7. Olympiakos and Panathinaikos compete in which country's top league?
   A: Turkey **B:** Greece **C:** Brazil

NATIONAL NICKNAMES

Match the national team's nickname with the team:

1. Les Bleus	Wales
2. Gli Azzurri	England
3. Oranje	Egypt
4. Y Dreigiau (The Dragons)	France
5. Die Mannschaft	South Africa
6. All Whites	Ireland
7. Socceroos	USA
8. Reggae Boyz	Turkey
9. Stars & Stripes	Australia
10. The Pharaohs	Netherlands
11. Bafana Bafana	Germany
12. The Desert Warriors	New Zealand
13. Na Buachaillí i Nglas (The Boys in Green)	Italy
14. Ay Yıldızlılar (The Crescent-Stars)	Jamaica
15. The Three Lions	Algeria

KITS

1. Tottenham Hotspur and Leeds United both wear which colour shirts for their home kit?
A: Red **B:** Blue **C:** White

2. Aston Villa and West Ham United both play in what colour combination for their home kit?
A: Red and White **B:** Claret and Blue **C:** Yellow and Black

3. Barcelona play in which iconic combination of stripes on their home shirts?
A: Red and Blue **B:** Blue and White **C:** Red and Black

4. Argentina wear which famous combination of stripes on their home shirts?
   A: White and Black **B:** White and Sky Blue
   C: White and Red

5. What colour was England's traditional away kit until 2011?
   A: Red **B:** White **C:** Blue

6. The Netherlands play in which colour at home?
   A: Blue **B:** Purple **C:** Orange

7. Brazil's home jersey is yellow, but what colour is the trim and numbers on the back?
   A: Blue **B:** Green **C:** Black

WAGS

Match the WAG or former WAG to the player:

1. Peter Crouch	Louise Nurding
2. David Beckham	Perrie Edwards
3. Jamie Redknapp	Cheryl Tweedy
4. Ashley Cole	Abbey Clancy
5. Alex Oxlade-Chamberlain	Shakira
6. Wayne Rooney	Victoria Adams
7. Gerard Piqué	Coleen McLoughlin

WORLD CUP

1. During which World Cup was the Mexican wave first broadcast to a worldwide audience?
   A: 1986 **B:** 1998 **C:** 2006

2. Which England goalkeeper made an incredible save, often dubbed 'the save of the century', to deny Pelé in the 1970 World Cup group stages?
   A: Gordon Canal **B:** Gordon Rivers **C:** Gordon Banks

3. Which player did David Beckham kick out at after being fouled in England's last-16 match against Argentina at the World Cup in 1998?
   A: Diego Costa **B:** Diego Simeone **C:** Diego Maradona

4. Which is the only country to have qualified for every World Cup?
   A: England **B:** Brazil **C:** Japan

5. The 1966 World Cup Final took place at which stadium?
   A: Wembley **B:** Rose Bowl, USA **C:** Stade de France

6. What was the name of the trophy presented to winners of the World Cup from 1930 to 1970?
   A: Jules Rimet **B:** Rodolphe Seeldrayers **C:** Arthur Drewry

RONALDO

1. Cristiano Ronaldo plays for which national team?
   A: Spain **B:** Portugal **C:** Brazil

2. Ronaldo is known by which nickname?
   A: CR7 **B:** Ron1 **C:** Christ7

3. Cristiano Ronaldo International Airport can be found on which island, where he was born?
   A: Sicily **B:** Isle of Man **C:** Madeira

4. Which Spanish club did Cristiano Ronaldo play for between 2009 and 2018?
   A: Barcelona **B:** Real Madrid **C:** Atlético Madrid

5. Ronaldo winked at his team's dugout after which English player and club teammate was sent off in the quarter-final of the 2006 World Cup?
   A: Rio Ferdinand **B:** Wayne Rooney **C:** Gary Neville

6. Which Italian club did Ronaldo join in 2018?
   A: Juventus **B:** Atalanta **C:** Lazio

7. Who did Ronaldo meet and present with a shirt featuring number 91 on the back, representing the person's age, before the 2010 World Cup?
   A: Pelé **B:** Nelson Mandela **C:** Muhammad Ali

MESSI

1. Lionel Messi plays for which national team?
   A: Argentina **B:** Brazil **C:** Italy

2. Lionel Messi joined which Spanish club aged just 13?
   A: Real Madrid **B:** Sevilla **C:** Barcelona

3. Messi has won which individual award a record six times?
   A: Ballon d'Or **B:** BBC Sports Personality World Sport Star of the Year **C:** PFA Player of the Year

4. Which sportswear company has sponsored Messi since 2006?
   A: Lonsdale **B:** Diadora **C:** Adidas

5. According to *Forbes*, Messi became the highest paid athlete in the world in 2019, earning approximately how much in salary, winnings and endorsements?
   A: $1.27 million **B:** $12.7 million **C:** $127 million

6. Which player is Messi describing here back in 2010? 'Even if I played for a million years, I'd never come close to ________________, not that I'd want to anyway. He's the greatest there's ever been.'
   A: George Best **B:** Diego Maradona **C:** Johan Cruyff

7. Messi was found guilty of which crime in July 2016, handed a 21-month suspended prison sentence and ordered to pay a reported £1.7 million fine?
   A: Tax Fraud **B:** Grand Theft Auto **C:** Piracy

BECKHAM

1. David Beckham wore which number on his shirt at Manchester United?
   A: 7 **B:** 8 **C:** 9

2. Which Major League Soccer club did David Beckham join in July 2007 from Real Madrid?
   A: LA Galaxy **B:** FC Cincinnati **C:** Austin FC

3. Which team did Beckham score a last-minute free kick against to ensure England qualified for the 2002 World Cup?
   A: Algeria **B:** Greece **C:** Australia

4. Which charity has David Beckham been an ambassador for since 2005?
   A: UNICEF UK **B:** Oxfam **C:** Samaritans

5. Which city was David Beckham born in?
   A: Edinburgh **B:** Belfast **C:** London

6. Which manager gave Becks the 'hairdryer treatment' back in 2003, culminating in him kicking a stray boot which struck Beckham above his eye and left him needing stitches?
   A: Vicente del Bosque **B:** Sir Alex Ferguson
   C: Sven-Göran Eriksson

7. Against which country did Beckham score a decisive penalty at the World Cup in 2002 that gave England a 1–0 victory?
   A: Spain **B:** Germany **C:** Argentina

WORLD'S RICHEST CLUBS

Can you put the 15 richest clubs in the world in 2021 (as recorded in the Deloitte Football Money League) in the correct order from the clues below?

1. Lionel Messi is this club's highest scorer of all time.
2. The club David Beckham left Man Utd to join.
3. South German giants and Champions League winners in 2020.
4. Wayne Rooney and Sir Bobby Charlton are this club's top scorers.
5. The red half of Merseyside.
6. Premier League champions in 2019.
7. The club Neymar Jr left Barcelona for.
8. Roman Abramovich has owned this London club since 2003.
9. Harry Kane joined this London club in 2009.
10. Italian club which means 'youth' in Italian.
11. London club based at the Emirates Stadium.
12. North German giants who Jürgen Klopp used to manage.
13. The red and white half of Spain's capital.
14. North Italian club based at the San Siro Stadium.
15. Biggest club in Russia's second city.

Arsenal
Manchester United
Atlético Madrid
Bayern Munich
Zenit St Petersburg
Liverpool
Manchester City
Tottenham Hotspur
Paris Saint-Germain
Inter Milan
Real Madrid
Borussia Dortmund
Juventus
Barcelona
Chelsea

CLUB NICKNAMES

Match the club nickname to the football club:

1. Gunners	Man Utd
2. Seagulls	Southampton
3. Owls	Millwall
4. Rams	Stoke City
5. Foxes	AFC Wimbledon
6. Red Devils	Brighton
7. Reds	Celtic
8. Blades	Rangers
9. Eagles	Arsenal
10. Saints	Leicester City
11. Hammers	Crystal Palace
12. Toffees	Portsmouth
13. Royals	Cardiff City
14. Magpies	West Ham United
15. Baggies	Reading
16. Pompey	Everton
17. Gers	Newcastle United
18. Bhoys	Sheffield United
19. Wombles	Liverpool
20. Bluebirds	Sheffield Wednesday
21. Lions	Derby County
22. Potters	West Bromwich Albion

WORLD CUP-WINNING NATIONS

Can you work out which World Cup-winning nations the clues below refer to?

1. The Costa Brava and Costa del Sol are found in this country.
2. You'll find the Colosseum here.
3. Porsche and BMW are car manufacturers associated with this country.
4. The home of samba.

5. Diego Maradona and Lionel Messi come from this place.
6. Winners of the 2018 World Cup.

DERBIES

1. Who are the two teams that compete in the Old Firm derby?
2. Which two teams compete in the East Anglian derby (also known as the Old Farm derby)?
3. The North London derby involves which two teams?
4. The Black Country derby features which two clubs?
5. The Merseyside derby involves which two clubs?
6. The M23 derby features which two teams?
7. Who contests the Tyne–Tees derby?
8. Which city is home to the clubs Heart of Midlothian (Hearts) and Hibernian?

TRIVIA

1. Which player gained the nickname 'Golden Balls'?
   A: Michael Owen **B:** David Beckham
   C: Cristiano Ronaldo

2. England won the World Cup in which year?
   A: 1966 **B:** 1976 **C:** 1986

3. Thierry Henry is a player most associated with which English football club?
   A: Chelsea **B:** Manchester Utd **C:** Arsenal

4. The letters QPR stand for what?
   A: Queen's Polo Regatta **B:** Queens Park Rangers
   C: Queen's Preston Royals

5. Which team has won the World Cup the most times?
   A: Netherlands **B:** Spain **C:** Brazil

6. Zinedine Zidane played for which country?
   A: France **B:** Brazil **C:** Spain

7. What is the top league in English football called?
   A: Super League **B:** Major League **C:** Premier League

8. How many lions feature on the England football badge?
   A: One **B:** Two **C:** Three

9. In Germany it's called an 'elfmeter'; what's it known as in England?
   A: A penalty kick **B:** A handball **C:** A throw-in

10. The expression 'squeaky bum time', referring to the sound made when anxiously moving around in a plastic seat while under pressure, is associated with which football manager?
    A: José Mourinho **B:** Sir Alex Ferguson
    C: Gareth Southgate

11. Who did England lose to in a penalty shoot-out in the semi-finals of the 1990 World Cup?
    A: West Germany **B:** France **C:** Argentina

12. Who knocked England out of the 2018 World Cup in extra time?
    A: Montenegro **B:** Serbia **C:** Croatia

13. Which footballer was nicknamed Gazza?
    A: Gary Lineker **B:** Paul Gascoigne **C:** Gary Neville

14. Which German team did Manchester United beat in 1999 to win the Champions League?
    A: Bayern Munich **B:** Eintracht Frankfurt **C:** RB Leipzig

15. Claudio Ranieri won the Premier League in 2016 managing which club, who were 5,000–1 outsiders at the beginning of the season?
    A: Aston Villa **B:** West Ham United **C:** Leicester City

16. The football highlights show *Match of the Day* first aired in which decade?
    A: 1930s **B:** 1960s **C:** 1990s

17. Which football club plays at the London Stadium, which was constructed for the London 2012 Olympics?
A: Millwall **B:** West Ham **C:** Crystal Palace

18. Which player has scored the most goals in the Premier League?
A: Alan Shearer **B:** Harry Kane **C:** Michael Owen

19. Extra time lasts how many minutes?
A: 20 minutes **B:** 30 minutes **C:** 45 minutes

20. Who won the Golden Boot for scoring the most goals at the World Cup in 2018?
A: Harry Kane **B:** Neymar Jr **C:** Fernando Torres

21. In 2018, England won a penalty shoot-out for the first time at a World Cup Finals, but who did they triumph against?
A: Ecuador **B:** Venezuela **C:** Colombia

22. 'You'll Never Walk Alone' is associated with which club?
A: Manchester City **B:** Chelsea **C:** Liverpool

23. Who is England's football manager, as at September 2021?
A: Steve Bould **B:** Gareth Southgate **C:** Rio Ferdinand

24. The World Cup in 2022 is due to take place in which country?
A: United Arab Emirates **B:** Qatar **C:** Oman

25. UEFA is football's governing body for which continent?
A: Europe **B:** North America **C:** South America

26. Which footballer famously said 'Just to confirm to all my followers I have had a hair transplant. I was going bald at 25. Why not?' on Twitter in 2011?
A: David Beckham **B:** Ryan Giggs **C:** Wayne Rooney

27. Which Scottish club was officially liquidated in 2012, owing a significant sum to HMRC?
A: Hibernian **B:** Hearts **C:** Rangers

28. Which former footballer took over as presenter of *Match of the Day* in 1999?
A: Gary Lineker **B:** Ian Wright **C:** Gareth Southgate

29. Which player was sold for approximately £198 million in 2017, a figure which broke the world transfer record?
A: Gareth Bale **B:** Neymar Jr **C:** Lionel Messi

30. Which England player scored a hat-trick in the 6–1 win over Panama at the 2018 World Cup?
A: Raheem Sterling **B:** Jamie Vardy **C:** Harry Kane

31. Which musical trio began their collaboration at an event in Rome on the eve of the 1990 World Cup Final?
A: The Three Tenors **B:** The Three Basses
C: The Three Sopranos

32. Who became the first foreign manager of the England national team in January 2001?
A: Fabio Capello **B:** Sven-Göran Eriksson
C: José Mourinho

33. George Best represented which national team?
A: Wales **B:** Scotland **C:** Northern Ireland

34. What does the abbreviation AET stand for?
A: Arsenal's Equalizer Tactics **B:** After Extra Time
C: Association of English Trainers

FOOTBALL (MEDIUM)

HARD MEN

Can you identify the legendary 'hard men' of football from the clues?

1. Despite suffering what turned out to be a broken leg, this legendary left back put his boot back on and told manager Harry Redknapp 'I'll give it a go' before the second half against Watford in 1999.
2. This bandaged, blood-spattered England captain went above and beyond to help secure England's qualification for Italia 90 against Sweden.
3. 'Razor' broke both of Andy Cole's legs during a tackle in a reserve game in 1996.
4. This defensive midfielder, nicknamed 'The Lawnmower', spent three years at Man City from 2009 to 2012 but may be best known for his kung-fu kick in the 2010 World Cup Final.
5. Bald enforcer nicknamed 'Mad Dog' who left Everton for Real Madrid in 2005 where he knocked out one of Ronaldo's teeth in training.
6. This Belgian rock at the back suffered what would later be determined to be a broken nose and a cracked eye socket but still played the last 60 minutes of a game against Serbia in 2013.
7. Possibly the craziest of 'The Crazy Gang', this midfielder nearly ripped off Gazza's crown jewels in 1988.
8. Combative striker, infamously nicknamed 'Disorderly', who fought off two burglars breaking into his house in 2001.

9. Former striker turned manager who lost his front teeth in his first appearance in a Leeds United shirt and was involved in a pitch-side altercation with Gennaro Gattuso in 2011.
10. This Chelsea legend in the sixties and seventies was famously nicknamed 'Chopper'.
11. Martin Keown once said of this no-nonsense Luton No. 9 and later Crazy Gang member: 'He once hit me so hard, I had to have a nerve taken out of my tooth.'
12. 'Invincibles' captain who was involved in a memorable bust-up in the Highbury tunnel in 2005 with the Man Utd captain.
13. Involved in a horror tackle on Alf-Inge Håland in 2001.
14. Stoke City club captain from 2010 to 2021, this centre back helped make the Britannia the stuff of nightmares for Arsenal.
15. German legend who once played on with a broken collarbone and dislocated shoulder in a World Cup semi-final in Mexico 1970.

GAFFERS' NICKNAMES

Match the nicknames to the managers:

1. The Special One	Antonio Conte
2. The Tinker Man	Arsène Wenger
3. The Wally with the Brolly	Claudio Ranieri
4. The Godfather	Pep Guardiola
5. Le Professeur	José Mourinho
6. The Exceptional One	Steve McClaren

DEADLINE DAY DEALS

Everyone loves a last-minute deal and rumours about players 'choppering in' to their new clubs, none more so than talkSPORT's king of transfer day Jim White. Can you identify the player(s) involved in the following transfers?

1. Which two players made headlines around the world when they signed in 2006 for West Ham United from Corinthians?
2. Who moved to a rival London club in 2006 for an unusual swap deal involving £5 million plus William Gallas?
3. Which player, who Chelsea manager Claudio Ranieri claimed would be the 'battery' of their team, signed from Real Madrid in 2003?
4. Who left his boyhood club in 2004 for Manchester Utd, where he would wear the No. 8 shirt?
5. Which striker was sat in a McDonald's in Northolt reportedly tucking into a Big Mac while waiting to learn his fate on deadline day in 2011 before being sold to Stoke City for an initial fee of £10 million?
6. Who left Liverpool in 2011 for £50 million on deadline day, breaking the then British transfer record?
7. Who joined Liverpool from Ajax in 2010 for a fee of £22.8 million?
8. And finally, which manager famously walked out of an interview in 2010 after he was referred to as 'a wheeler and dealer' in reference to his history of last-minute signings?

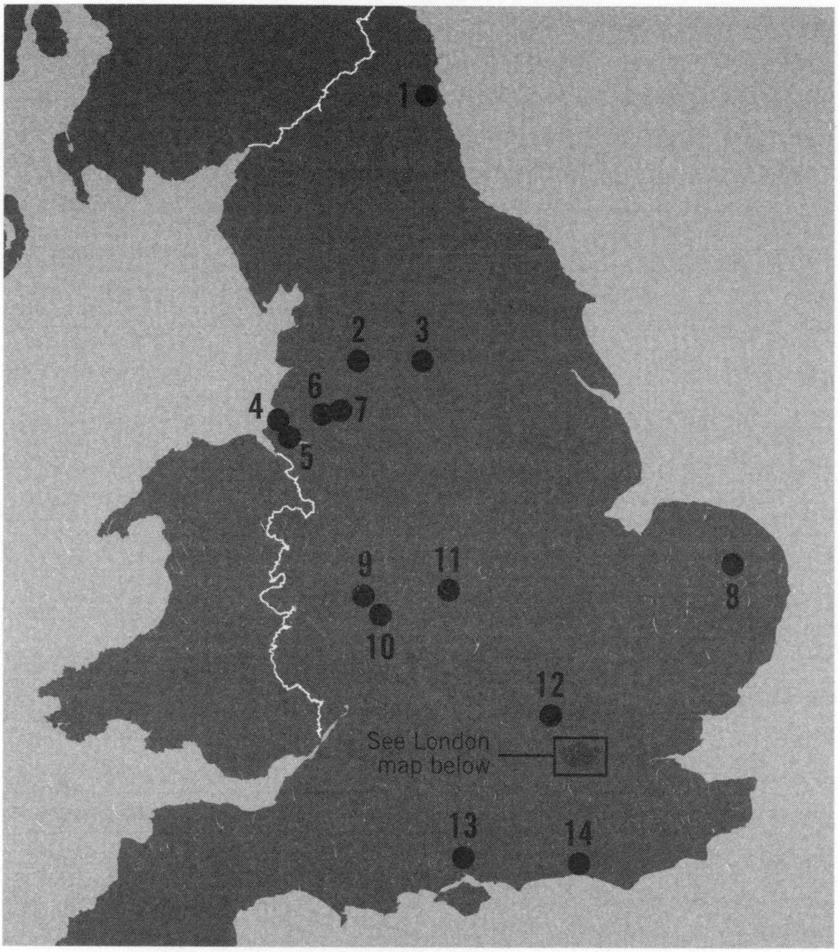

1
2
3
6
4
7
5
9
11
8
10
12
See London map below
13
14

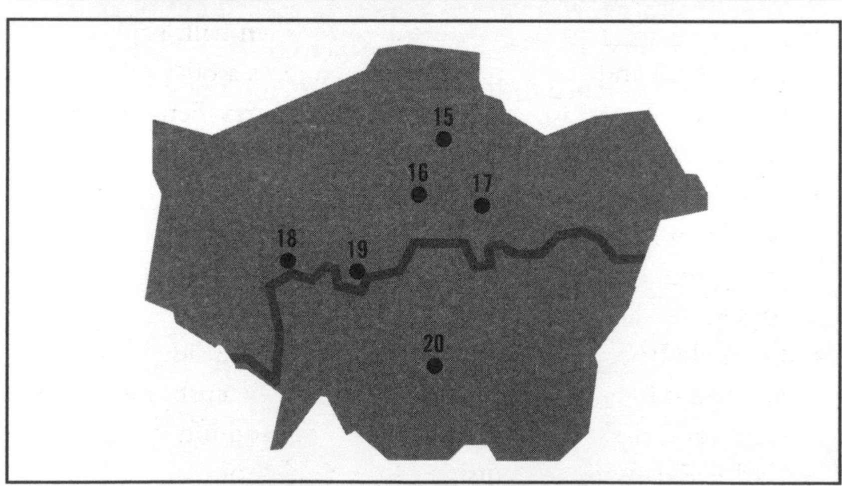

WHERE ARE YER?

Hope you remember your GCSE Geography! Match the numbers on the map opposite to the Premier League football clubs below.

Arsenal
Aston Villa
Brentford
Brighton & Hove Albion
Burnley
Chelsea
Crystal Palace
Everton
Leeds United
Leicester City
Liverpool
Manchester City
Manchester United
Newcastle United
Norwich City
Southampton
Tottenham Hotspur
Watford
West Ham United
Wolverhampton Wanderers

WONDER GOALS

Who scored the wonder goals described below?

1. David Beckham finds ______________ in the centre circle. He sprints past José Chamot, pushes the ball past Roberto Ayala and into the right-hand side of the penalty area before striking the ball high and across the keeper Carlos Roa.
2. ____________ picks up the ball in his own half, spins past Peter Reid and Peter Beardsley, and begins a 60-yard dash, taking on Terry Butcher, sprinting past Terry Fenwick and taking the ball around Peter Shilton before slotting it in.
3. Arnold Mühren plays a deep cross to the far right of the penalty area, which _________ takes on the volley, thumping it over keeper Rinat Dasayev from the tightest of angles.
4. Frank de Boer launches a 60-yard ball from inside his own half towards ________________, which he cushions with his right foot, flicks it inside Roberto Ayala and lifts it past Carlos Roa with the outside of his right foot.

5. Joe Hart tries to clear a long-ball forward with a weak looping header, which _______________ sends over his head with a 30-yard angled bicycle kick.
6. Pelé touches the ball to Clodoaldo inside his own half who skips past four Italian challenges before laying it off to Rivelino. Rivelino arrows a down-the-line pass to Jairzinho, who comes inside and rolls a pass along to Pelé, who casually lays it off to the onrushing _______________, who rifles a drive into the bottom left corner.

MATCH THE CLUB TO THE COUNTRY

All the clubs below have performed in the Champions League. But can you match up the clubs to the countries they belong to?

1. Maccabi Haifa
2. Heerenveen
3. Trabzonspor
4. Red Star Belgrade
5. Genk
6. Young Boys
7. FC Copenhagen
8. CFR Cluj
9. Helsingborg
10. Sturm Graz
11. Sparta Prague
12. Rubin Kazan
13. Shakhtar Donetsk
14. Molde
15. Dinamo Zagreb
16. Legia Warsaw
17. Levski Sofia
18. Debrecen
19. Maribor
20. Qarabağ
21. BATE Borisov
22. Astana
23. Panathinaikos
24. Braga
25. 1899 Hoffenheim
26. Celta Vigo
27. Lens
28. Atalanta

Greece
Denmark
Sweden
Hungary
Norway
Croatia
Russia
Bulgaria
Germany
France
Poland
Italy

Spain
Kazakhstan
Portugal
Netherlands
Belgium
Turkey
Serbia
Switzerland

Romania
Israel
Slovenia
Azerbaijan
Belarus
Ukraine
Czech Republic
Austria

CHANTS FROM THE TERRACES

1. At which club did the chant 'No one likes us, we don't care' originate during the 1970s?
2. With which club is the song 'Marching on Together' associated?
3. With which club is the song 'Blue Moon' linked?
4. Which club's home ground does the song 'I'm Forever Blowing Bubbles' ring around?
5. Fill in the missing player's name from the following Arsenal chant around 2014: 'Podolski to the left of me, Walcott to the right, here I am, stuck in the middle _______'
6. Guess this one from the Kop circa 2007: 'He's big, he's red, his feet stick out of bed, ______________'
7. Who are these unkind but amusing Fulham fans singing about, to the tune of Dean Martin's 'That's Amore' around 2009? 'When you're sat in row Z, and the ball hits your head, that's __________'
8. At which club did this anthem ring out, to the tune of 'Happy Days', after defender Habib Beye impressed the home fans in 2007–2008? 'Sunday, Monday Habib Beye; Tuesday, Wednesday Habib Beye; Thursday, Friday Habib Beye; Saturday, Habib Beye, rocking all week with you!'

PREMIER LEAGUE HAT-TRICKS

Fill in the players who have scored the most Premier League hat-tricks from the clues we've kindly provided.

PLAYER	Number of hat-tricks	First hat-trick	Most recent hat-trick	Club(s) scored for
	12	10/9/2011	12/01/2020	Man City
	11	23/10/1993	19/09/1999	Blackburn Rovers, Newcastle Utd
	9	30/10/1993	26/12/2001	Liverpool, Leeds Utd
	8	26/12/2000	07/05/2006	Arsenal
	8	21/03/2015	26/12/2017	Tottenham Hotspur
	8	14/02/1998	17/12/2005	Liverpool, Newcastle Utd
	7	28/10/2006	29/11/2017	Man Utd, Everton
	6	28/04/2012	22/03/2014	Liverpool
	5	29/12/2007	26/12/2011	Tottenham Hotspur, Man Utd
	5	22/01/2011	22/04/2013	Arsenal, Man Utd
	5	22/12/2001	27/09/2003	Man Utd
	5	21/11/1993	30/08/1999	Newcastle Utd, Man Utd
	5	05/03/1994	13/12/1997	Arsenal

FIVE FAMOUS FREE KICKS

1. __________ catches ponytailed keeper David Seaman off guard with a curling free kick into the top left corner in the 2002 World Cup quarter-final.
2. _________ spends a few seconds placing the ball down, walks 18 steps backwards before beginning his characteristic staccato run-up, finally breaking into a sprint and sending a physics-defying rocket off the right post and past Fabien Barthez in the first game of the 1997 Tournoi de France.
3. It's the 93rd minute in a European qualifier in 2001 with England trailing 2–1. ________________ steps up with a curling free kick that buries itself in the top left corner.
4. _________, in his characteristic stance, stands square-on to the ball with his legs wide apart before sending an unstoppable knuckleball free kick that starts straightish before bending sharply past Portsmouth's David James and into the top right corner.
5. Jim Magilton rolls an indirect free kick backwards towards ______________, who tees the ball up with his right foot before unleashing a perfect dipping volley past Wimbledon goalkeeper Hans Segers.

WHO'S HE ON ABOUT?

Match the legend to the quote about him:

Ronaldinho	Sir Bobby Charlton	Gianluigi Buffon
Diego Maradona	Zinedine Zidane	Andrés Iniesta
Neymar Jr	Cristiano Ronaldo	Franz Beckenbauer
Roberto Carlos	Johan Cruyff	Pelé
Kylian Mbappé	Thierry Henry	Alessandro Del Piero

1. Paul Pogba: '__________________ has much more talent than I have. Do you see what he is doing at his age? No, I never had his talent.'

2. Terry Venables: 'Was he the greatest European player of all time? On form, it's difficult to imagine who was better. It does not matter how and where you remember _______________ playing, he was the best; in midfield he was the best; deep, the best; as an attacker, the best.'
3. Ryan Giggs: 'I think he just epitomises Manchester United. He was one of the best players there's ever been and he's someone who is humble, approachable and who oozes class. He's a great person to know and he's someone who has inspired me and helped me throughout my career.'
4. Rio Ferdinand in 2017: 'He's the heir to the throne of Cristiano Ronaldo and Messi.'
5. Pelé (talking about this player's retirement in 2018): 'You brought a smile to everyone's face. It was impossible to love football and not be your fan. Thank you for the show. I hope you glide through life, like you glided through tackles.'
6. Martin Keown: 'I do remember saying to him when he scored his first goal, 'I'll be able to tell my kids I played with you, and I meant every word of it.'
7. Zlatan Ibrahimović: 'When ___________________ stepped onto the pitch, the 10 other guys just got suddenly better. It is that simple. It was magic. He was a unique player. He was more than good, he came from another planet. His team-mates became like him when he was on the pitch.'
8. Gary Lineker: 'When _______________ scored that second goal against us, I felt like applauding. I'd never felt like that before, but it's true … and not just because it was such an important game. It was impossible to score such a beautiful goal. He's the greatest player of all time, by a long way. A genuine phenomenon.'
9. Petr Čech: 'Oliver Kahn, Peter Schmeichel and Edwin van der Sar inspired me early in my career. Then ___________ appeared and changed everything.'
10. Xavi: '__________ is easily Spain's most complete player. He has everything. Playing alongside him is very easy.'

11. Jaap Stam: 'His left leg seems to be made of iron. He had a fantastic shot, but thankfully I have never stood in the wall when he took a free kick.'
12. Ferenc Puskás: 'The greatest player in history was Di Stefano. I refuse to classify __________ as a player. He was above that.'
13. Francesco Totti: '… what an opponent! What a player! What a person! A real symbol, a champion who gave trophies to the Juventus fans, he loves that shirt and gives lots of back pain to opposing goalkeepers.'
14. Sir Alex Ferguson: 'After we played Sporting last week, the lads in the dressing room talked about him constantly, and on the plane back from the game they urged me to sign him. That's how highly they rated him.'
15. Sir Bobby Charlton: '__________ was a marvellous distributor of the ball, a great tackler, he always had control of a situation and he never panicked. He was extremely cool and never looked like he was at full stretch. Such a hard player to play against.'

PLAYERS' NICKNAMES

Match the nickname to the players:

1. Baby-faced Assassin	Darren Anderton
2. The Guv'nor	David Beckham
3. Non-flying Dutchman	Tony Adams
4. Chicharito (Little Pea)	Stuart Pearce
5. Il Divino Codino (The Divine Ponytail)	George Best
6. Sick Note	Ole Gunnar Solskjær
7. Psycho	Javier Hernández
8. Golden Balls	Ray Parlour
9. The Fifth Beatle	Dennis Bergkamp
10. Mr Arsenal	Paul Ince
11. Romford Pelé	Roberto Baggio

MASCOTS

Match the Premier League mascots to their clubs. In case you're wondering why there are only 19, Everton are currently in mascot limbo!

1. Arsenal	Bertie Bee
2. Aston Villa	Moonchester
3. Brentford	Kop Cat
4. Brighton & Hove Albion	Wolfie and Wendy
5. Burnley	Sammy Saint
6. Chelsea	Buzz and Buzzette
7. Crystal Palace	Fred the Red
8. Leeds United	Hammerhead
9. Leicester City	Chirpy
10. Liverpool	Monty Magpie
11. Manchester City	Hercules the Lion
12. Manchester United	Pete the Eagle
13. Newcastle United	Mighty Red
14. Norwich City	Harry the Hornet
15. Southampton	Gunnersaurus
16. Tottenham Hotspur	Filbert Fox
17. Watford	Captain Canary
18. West Ham United	Stamford and Bridget the Lion
19. Wolverhampton Wanderers	Gully the Seagull

POST-MATCH MAGIC

Which managers made the following legendary quotes after a game?

1. This former West Bromwich Albion and Manchester United manager came up with this cracker after West Brom lost in the 1979 UEFA Cup quarter-final: 'I never comment on referees and I'm not going to break the habit of a lifetime for that prat.'

2. This immortal line was uttered by the victorious manager after the dramatic end to the 1999 Champions League final: 'Football, bloody hell.'
3. The new Arsenal manager won many new fans after this classic in 1996: 'I tried to watch the Tottenham match on television in my hotel yesterday, but I fell asleep.'
4. A gem from this popular Italian manager in 2016: 'Football managers are like a parachutist, at times, it doesn't open. Here, it is an umbrella. You understand, Mary Poppins.'
5. We think this one's a complaint about time-wasting, but only this title-winning Chelsea manager will know for sure: 'You may as well put a cow in the middle of the pitch, walking. And then stop the game because there was a cow.'
6. One from a bubble-permed Liverpool, Newcastle and England forward turned manager: 'They're the second-best team in the world, and there's no higher praise than that.'
7. A classic from the West Ham gaffer about one of his own players in 1997: 'John Hartson's got more previous than Jack the Ripper.'
8. This QPR boss always was good value in a post-match press conference, as he showed after losing to Aston Villa in the English League Cup in 2004: 'We're like a bad tea-bag – we never stay in the cup that long.'
9. One from a legendary Liverpool manager between 1959 and 1974: 'This city has two great teams – Liverpool and Liverpool reserves.'
10. This iconic Nottingham Forest manager had a lot of qualities, but modesty might not have counted among them: 'I wouldn't say I was the best manager in the world. But I was in the top one.'

SAY WHAT?

Match the legendary quote to the player:

George Best
Wayne Rooney
Ian Rush
Eric Cantona
Michael Owen
Zlatan Ibrahimović
Paul Gascoigne
Mario Balotelli
John Barnes
Peter Crouch

1. 'When the seagulls follow the trawler, it's because they think sardines will be thrown into the sea.'
2. 'One thing is for sure, a World Cup without me is nothing to watch so it is not worthwhile to wait for the World Cup.'
3. 'I'm more afraid of my mum than Sven-Göran Eriksson or David Moyes.'
4. 'I spent a lot of money on booze, birds and fast cars. The rest I just squandered.'
5. 'They didn't get angry because I took my shirt off and got booked, they saw my physique and got jealous.'
6. 'The Brazilians were shocked, and I suppose that's why they didn't tackle me, because they thought there was no way an Englishman is going to do this.'
7. 'I don't have any tattoos, but that's mainly because none of my limbs are wide enough to support a visible image.'
8. 'I've had 14 bookings this season – eight of which were my fault, but seven of which were disputable.'
9. 'That would've been a goal had it gone inside the post.'
10. 'I couldn't settle in Italy. It was like living in a foreign country.'

MOST CAPPED ENGLAND PLAYERS

Use the clues to reveal the list of England's most capped players:

1. England goalkeeper from 1970 to 1990
2. England's record goalscorer
3. Became a Galáctico in 2003
4. Only played for two clubs: Liverpool and LA Galaxy
5. World Cup-winning captain
6. The left back from 'The Invincibles'
7. Ballon d'Or winner in 1966
8. Known as 'Super' at Stamford Bridge
9. Wolves legend and longest-serving England captain
10. Man Utd midfielder and later Middlesbrough manager

ENGLAND'S PENALTY PAIN

1. Not wishing to reopen old wounds, but which two England players missed penalties in the semi-finals of Italia 90 against West Germany?
2. Who missed the penalty that sent Germany through to the Euro 96 final?
3. Which two England players missed penalties in the round of 16 against Argentina at France 98?
4. Which two England players missed penalties in the quarter-finals of Euro 2004 against Portugal?
5. Which three England players missed penalties in Germany 2006?
6. Which two England players missed penalties in the quarter-finals of Euro 2012 against Italy?
7. And just so this segment isn't the most depressing thing in the book, which four England players scored their penalties in the victory (yes, you read right) against Spain in the quarter-finals of Euro 96?

WHO ARE YER?

Match the clubs with the names of their grounds:

1. Portsmouth	Riverside Stadium
2. West Bromwich Albion	Deepdale
3. Charlton Athletic	Fratton Park
4. Coventry City	Carrow Road
5. Millwall	Madejski Stadium
6. Norwich City	Meadow Lane
7. Sunderland	The Valley
8. Ipswich Town	Vicarage Road
9. Luton	Vitality Stadium
10. Reading	Portman Road
11. Watford	The Den
12. Preston North End	Loftus Road
13. Notts County	Ricoh Arena
14. Middlesbrough	The Hawthorns
15. QPR	Stadium of Light
16. Bournemouth	Kenilworth Road

ANAGRAMS

Sort out this Serie A mess and unscramble the names of the top-flight Italian teams:

1. LATIN MINER
2. OIL PAN
3. I ZOLA
4. SEED UNI
5. RADIO SPAM
6. ANOINT FIRE
7. NO RIOT
8. A RAMP
9. ANAL MIC
10. JET SUN UV

Untangle the names of the La Liga teams:

1. COBRA LANE
2. ADMIRAL DRE
3. LIL VASE
4. LIBERATES
5. NICE LAVA
6. LARVAL LIE
7. DICTATOR MAILED
8. ETHICAL BOBTAIL
9. ARCADE SOILED
10. SO SAUNA

OWN GOALS AND GAFFES

1. In 2009, Darren Bent scored a controversial goal via which large red object that had been launched onto the pitch?
2. Which defender scored a spectacular own goal in September 1991, curling the ball from 25 yards and over the head of David Seaman?
3. Which Irish defender, who played for Man City, Everton, Aston Villa and QPR, holds the unwanted record for most own goals (10) scored in the Premier League?
4. Which Liverpool player spectacularly missed a 10-yard tap-in against Aston Villa in 1992 after doing all the hard work and rounding the keeper?
5. Which striker famously sent the ball over the bar from one yard out playing for West Bromwich Albion against Middlesbrough in a must-win relegation battle in November 2004?

PREMIER LEAGUE RED CARDS

Using the clues below, can you work out the identity of the seven players who have been shown the most red cards in the history of the Premier League?

1. 1= (eight red cards) Irish former Man City captain
2. 1= (eight red cards) Scored more goals than any other Scot in the Premier League

3. 1= (eight red cards) Went from Arsenal to Juventus to Inter to Man City
4. 4= (seven red cards) Played 280 games for Sunderland between 2009 and 2019
5. 4= (seven red cards) Played Big Chris in *Lock, Stock and Two Smoking Barrels* after his retirement
6. 4= (seven red cards) Took over from Eric Cantona as Man Utd's club captain
7. 4= (seven red cards) Striker turned midfielder who left Leeds United to join Man Utd in 2004

IT'S NOT A QUESTION OF SPORT

It's Not a Question of Sport is a funny/occasionally infuriating game that closes out talkSPORT's late-night show 'The Sports Bar'. You've got to guess the names, in this case footballers, from a series of clues completely unrelated to sport that spell out their names (or something close to it!).

1. Organic matter used in gardening and making whisky
2. Two-letter word expressing hesitation
3. Sound you make when instructing someone to be quiet
4. What a singer sings into (short version)
5. Pretty low temperature

1. At the end of the …
2. Another word for a VHS, then shorten it to three letters
3. Something you enjoy with a bit of tonic
4. Say hello to your Spanish neighbours

1. Madonna sang about a ____ of light
2. Document you draw up near the end of life
3. Close family and relations
4. Chemical symbol for sulphur

QUESTIONS: FOOTBALL (MEDIUM)

1. The Greeks wangled their way into this city
2. Academic title for head of a faculty
3. When greeting in Yorkshire, you might say '____ up'

1. Stick your hand in the fire and you'll get a ____
2. Watch out for that fella, he's well _____
3. Female deer
4. Second place medal

1. Something you do to a petrol tank
2. Another word for enemy
3. Fox's home

1. French cocktail made with blackcurrant
2. Small crawly insect
3. Dangerous water current
4. Brighton, Bournemouth and Blackpool have got one

1. Postman Pat's cat
2. Big expanse of salt water
3. Suffix used to describe young swans and geese
4. Protect someone from harm

1. Fifth month
2. Like father, like ____
3. Something a photograph is set on for display

1. Knighthood
2. Greek word for Earth
3. Form of computer memory
4. 'I sat on the roof and kicked off the _____'

1. King of the jungle
2. Dante imagined nine circles in this place
3. One of the Mr Men, renowned for his untidiness

1. Line of seating in a cinema
2. Rough seedcase of a plant
3. Pull a broken-down vehicle
4. Slang for a criminal gang
5. Stingy person
6. Short word used to express surprise

1. Nick something
2. The French call it a 'poubelle'
3. UPS and FedEx turn up in one of these
4. A happy cat makes this sound
5. Jurisdiction of the bishop of Rome, the Holy ____

1. Cher likes walking in this US city
2. After you've got the bill, you've got ____

1. Polite word for a bog
2. La-di-dah is what a Cockney might call this
3. This lot weren't keen on rockers
4. Earning more than a few quid

1. Cornish eco tourist attraction
2. Venturing a guess

1. Young female horse
2. Three major battles were fought near this Belgian city
3. Water bird with a white patch above its beak
4. Adolescent
5. Slang American greeting often used by Rocky Balboa

1. Five guys named ____
2. Expression for overacting
3. Short form of the sea in southern Europe
4. Sounds a bit like a room in the bottom of your house

1. Something that happens to us all, alas
2. You got £200 for passing this place
3. Shortened form of mother
4. A skater's term of approval
5. Italian word for 'lady'

1. Don't park on the soft _____
2. Girl associated with climbing a hill
3. Transit, Transport, Camper
4. Drainage ditch

PREMIER LEAGUE CLUBS

Here's a tricky one that will earn you a proper pat on the back if you get them all. At the start of the 2021–2022 season a total of 50 clubs have competed in the Premier League. Can you get them all?

1. ____________	18. ____________	35. ____________
2. ____________	19. ____________	36. ____________
3. ____________	20. ____________	37. ____________
4. ____________	21. ____________	38. ____________
5. ____________	22. ____________	39. ____________
6. ____________	23. ____________	40. ____________
7. ____________	24. ____________	41. ____________
8. ____________	25. ____________	42. ____________
9. ____________	26. ____________	43. ____________
10. ____________	27. ____________	44. ____________
11. ____________	28. ____________	45. ____________
12. ____________	29. ____________	46. ____________
13. ____________	30. ____________	47. ____________
14. ____________	31. ____________	48. ____________
15. ____________	32. ____________	49. ____________
16. ____________	33. ____________	50. ____________
17. ____________	34. ____________	

SCOTTISH PREMIER LEAGUE

Sixteen clubs have played in the Scottish Premier League since its inception in the 2013–14 season. Name them! We've given you the first letter of each …

1. A __________	**7.** H __________	**13.** R __________
2. C __________	**8.** I __________	**14.** R __________
3. D __________	**9.** K __________	**15.** S __________
4. D __________	**10.** L __________	**16.** S __________
5. H __________	**11.** M __________	
6. H __________	**12.** P __________	

TRIVIA

1. What number did David Beckham wear on his shirt at Real Madrid and LA Galaxy?
2. Which disgraced FIFA president was ejected from office in 2015?
3. The Poznań celebration, in which fans turn their backs to the pitch, link arms and jump up and down in unison was imported by which English club after witnessing it performed by travelling Lech Poznań supporters?
4. Eric Cantona joined Manchester United in 1992 from which club?
5. In 2002, the FA controversially sanctioned the relocation of Wimbledon FC to which town?
6. In 2010, Man Utd fans began to wear which two colours as a sign of rebellion against the Glazer family?
7. Who loudly exclaimed 'Let's be having you!' over the PA system at half-time at Carrow Road in 2005 in an attempt to rally her beloved Norwich City?
8. Who is the Honorary Life-President of Watford FC?
9. Former Prime Minister David Cameron made a famous gaffe in 2015 saying he supported which club when he actually meant Aston Villa?

10. Which Serie A club did Beckham join on loan in 2009 and 2010?

11. Which manager was voted talkSPORT's Numpty of the Week in October 2020 for standing by while the club's diminutive Head of Media Relations Karen Shotbolt held an umbrella over his head after an away game at Brighton, recalling Steve McClaren back in 2008?

12. Which Brazilian player would have certainly won Numpty of the Week for falling to the ground clutching his head after Turkish player Hakan Unsal kicked the ball towards him towards the end of their first game of the 2002 World Cup?

FOOTBALL (HARD)

FOOTBALL LEAGUE AND NON-LEAGUE

1. In 2014, Salford City were taken over by which five former Man Utd players, who each took a 10% share in the club?
2. Which half of a legendary comedy duo served as vice president of Luton Town from 1975 until his death in 1984?
3. The Chuckle Brothers were made honorary presidents of which club in 2007?
4. Which 22-year-old boyband singer was due to take over Doncaster Rovers in 2014 before the deal fell through?
5. Which non-league club did Jamie Vardy leave to join Leicester in 2012?
6. Which four English clubs in either the Premier League or Football League wear orange or primarily orange for their home kit?

EFL AND PREMIER LEAGUE CLUBS

Each week, on talkSPORT's Weekend Sports Breakfast, we randomly select two clubs from the 92 professional teams in the EFL and Premier League, and we quiz Natalie Sawyer and Tony Cascarino on those clubs. Can you name the clubs from the clues?

1. Returned to the Premier League in 1998 after a 77-year absence from the top flight.
2. Jan Åge Fjørtoft was this club's top scorer in their one season in the Premier League.
3. This team plays their home games at Highbury Stadium.

4. Teddy Sheringham won Player of the Year for this club in 1991.
5. Hold the record for longest unbeaten run of league matches in English senior football.
6. Won the European Cup Winners' Cup in 1965 at Wembley.
7. This London club's crest features two red wyverns facing each other.
8. A 9ft high bronze statue of Brian Clough and Peter Taylor has pride of place outside this club's ground.
9. The most southerly and westerly club in the EFL.
10. The most easterly club in the EFL.

Can you name all these EFL clubs from the second part of their names?

1. Albion (x 3):
2. Athletic (x 3):
3. City (x 14):
4. County (x 2):
5. Rovers (x 5):
6. Town (x 11):
7. United (x 14):
8. Wanderers (x 3):

FIRST FOOTBALL LEAGUE CLUBS

Back in 1888, 12 clubs all from the Midlands and North of England participated in the first Football League. Can you name them? We've provided the first letters …

1. A ___________
2. A ___________
3. B ___________
4. B ___________
5. B ___________
6. D ___________
7. E ___________
8. N ___________
9. P ___________
10. S ___________
11. W ___________
12. W ___________

UNBELIEVABLE SCENES

1. The so-called Battle of Nuremberg, which took place at the 2006 World Cup and resulted in the sending off of four players and the issuing of 16 yellow cards, involved which teams?
2. Which goalkeeper was responsible for a horrific foul on defender Patrick Battiston in the 1982 World Cup semi-final between France and Germany that left Battiston unconscious?
3. A legendary 'non-handshake' occurred during a game between Chelsea and Manchester City in 2010, but which two players were involved?
4. Who did Zinedine Zidane head-butt in the 2006 World Cup Final?

HALFWAY LINE AND BEYOND

1. Who hit a 70-yard lob over tumbling Newcastle keeper Steven Harper at Anfield in 2011?
2. Who laced a drive from the centre circle over West Ham's Joe Hart to complete his hat-trick in 2017 for the boyhood club that he returned to after leaving Man Utd?
3. Who smacked a swiftly taken free kick from a couple of yards inside his own half over Stoke keeper Thomas Sorensen in 2009?
4. Who looped a strike from the halfway line over Wimbledon keeper Neil Sullivan on the opening day of the Premier League season in 1996?
5. Which keeper scored from inside his own penalty box at Goodison Park against Bolton in January 2012 with a little bit of help from the wind?
6. Which keeper scored after only 13 seconds of a game for Stoke against Southampton in 2013?
7. Who beat Chelsea's Thibaut Courtois from inside his own half for Stoke in 2015?

HISTORY MAKERS

1. Which Dutch legend pioneered a turn that is named after him?
2. Which cheeky penalty kick, named after the Czech midfielder who pioneered it in 1976, involves a player nonchalantly chipping the ball down the middle of the goal while the keeper dives to the left or right?
3. Which player is forever associated with a move involving holding the ball between both feet and 'hopping' through the air between two defenders?
4. Which goalkeeper pioneered the 'scorpion kick', performing it in a friendly between Colombia and England at Wembley in 1995?
5. Which player, who went on to pursue a career in Hollywood as an actor, earned the quickest yellow card, after three seconds, in Premier League history?
6. Which Scottish forward became the first player sold for a transfer fee of over £100,000 for his move from Torino to Man Utd in 1962?
7. Who became Britain's first £1 million player during his transfer from Birmingham City to Nottingham Forest in 1979?
8. As at August 2021, which player was responsible for the largest transfer fee paid by an English club to another English club?
9. Who became the world's most expensive goalkeeper in 2018 when he was sold by Athletic Bilbao?
10. Who became the world's most expensive teenager when he joined Paris Saint-Germain in 2017 for approximately €180 million?
11. In 2009, which Premier League goalkeeper set a new record of 1,311 minutes without conceding a goal?
12. Which goalkeeper scored four goals in the 2002 World Cup qualifiers for the South American zone (CONMEBOL), the same number as strikers Marcelo Salas, Iván Zamorano and Juan Pablo Ángel?

FILL IN THE TEAMS

It's the semi-finals of Euro 96 and England v Germany. Can you name the England starting line-up? One clue: Gary Neville was suspended so El Tel opted for a 3–5–2 formation.

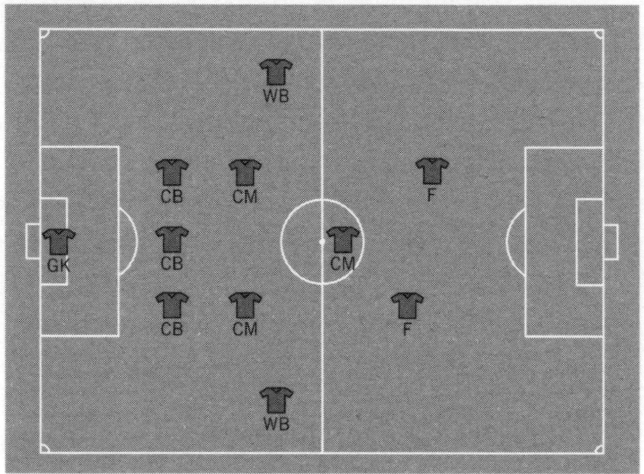

Arsenal fan or not, the 2003–04 Premier League season was one of the most incredible in English football history. Can you name the Invincibles' most-used line-up?

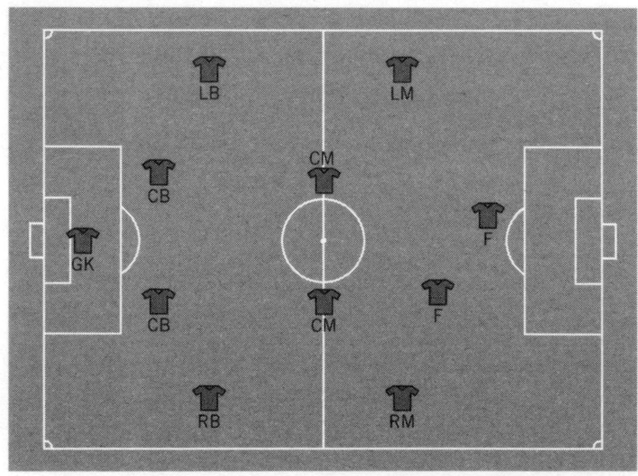

The Champions League Final of 2008 was the first all-English final in the history of the competition. Can you name the starting XIs?

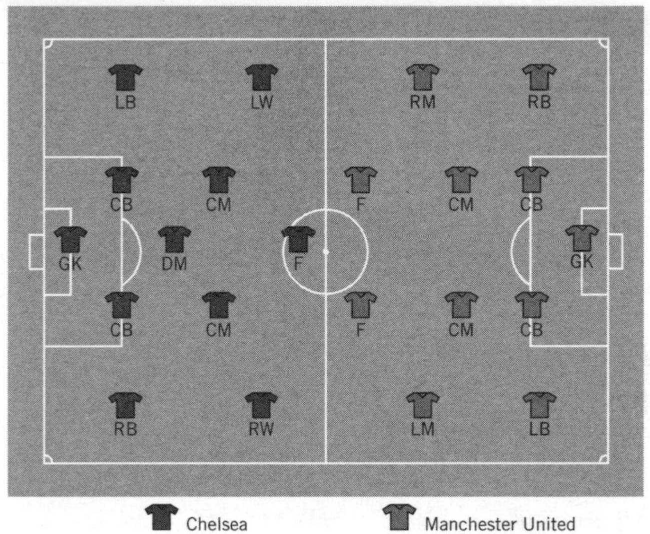

On the last day of the 2011–12 Premier League season, Man City clinched the title by scoring two stoppage-time goals against QPR to win 3–2 and break the hearts of their arch-rivals across town. Can you remember the Man City line-up?

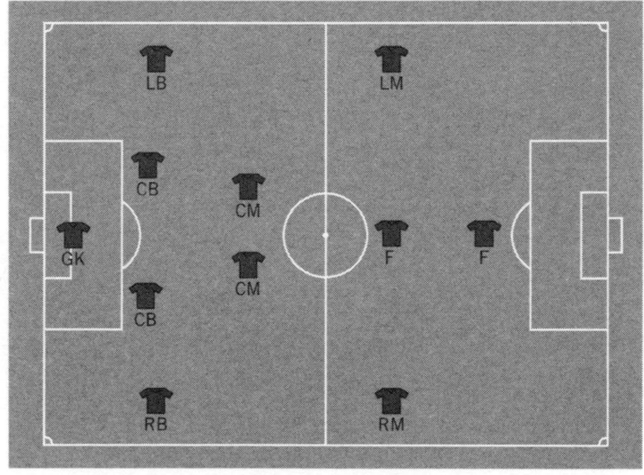

SHIRT SPONSORS

Taking you back to the first season of the Premier League, in 1992–1993, can you match the shirt sponsor to the club?

1. Arsenal	ICI
2. Aston Villa	Peugeot
3. Blackburn Rovers	Draper Tools
4. Chelsea	No shirt sponsor
5. Coventry City	Classic FM
6. Crystal Palace	Tulip Computers
7. Everton	J-D Sports
8. Ipswich Town	Sanderson
9. Leeds United	Admiral Sportswear
10. Liverpool	Carlsberg
11. Man City	Laver
12. Man Utd	Holsten
13. Middlesbrough	JVC
14. Nottingham Forest	Norwich and Peterborough Building Society
15. Norwich City	Labatt's
16. Oldham Athletic	NEC
17. QPR	Mita Copiers
18. Sheffield United	Brother
19. Sheffield Wednesday	Fisons
20. Southampton	McEwan's Lager
21. Tottenham Hotspur	Sharp
22. Wimbledon	Commodore

It's the turn of the millennium. Can you match the shirt sponsors to the clubs?

1. Arsenal	Walkers Crisps
2. Aston Villa	Autoglass
3. Bradford	Reg Vardy
4. Chelsea	LDV Vans
5. Coventry City	Carlsberg

6. Derby County	Phones4U
7. Everton	Dr Martens
8. Leeds United	Holsten
9. Leicester City	Subaru
10. Liverpool	Dreamcast
11. Man Utd	Sanderson
12. Middlesbrough	BT Cellnet
13. Newcastle United	Friends Provident
14. Sheffield Wednesday	Sharp
15. Southampton	Newcastle Brown Ale
16. Sunderland	JCT600
17. Tottenham Hotspur	Tiny
18. Watford	EDC
19. West Ham United	One2One
20. Wimbledon	Packard Bell

CHARISMATIC CHAIRMEN AND OWNERS

1. Who lived up to his agreement to kiss striker Dean Holdsworth's bare bum if he scored over 15 goals in the 1993–94 Premier League season?
2. Which chairman became the owner of Cardiff City in May 2010 and attempted to change their home strip from blue to red and alter their bluebird badge to a red dragon?
3. Which club owner said of his own club in 2019 'I'm a negative to that football club … I didn't just shoot myself in the foot; I blew my own leg off.'
4. Which chairman said: 'At the end of the day, I have a certain hairstyle. Whether I'm too old to carry it off now, I'm not sure. But it's a subject for discussion, and there's only one thing worse than people talking about you – and that's people not talking about you.'

5. Who said: 'I got calls from Italy last summer and one agent offered me [Gabriel] Batistuta. He told me, "Batistuta wants to come to Chelsea." I said, "I'm sure he does, but we've stopped signing pensioners."'
6. 'I feel like the guy who shot Bambi. I'm not an egotistical loony.' Which chairman said this in 1993 after giving a popular Spurs manager the sack?

LATIN MOTTOS

Latin mottos have mostly disappeared from club badges but several remain and a couple are so tied up with the history of the club that they're still very well known by their fans. Can you match the mottos with the clubs?

1. *Arte et Labore* (By Skill and Labour)
2. *Audere est Facere* (To Dare Is to Do)
3. *Nil Satis Nisi Optimum* (Nothing but the Best is Good Enough)
4. *Consilio et Anamis* (Intelligence and Courage)
5. *Vincit Omnia Industria* (Hard Work Conquers All)
6. *Consectatio Excellentiae* (In Pursuit of Excellence)
7. *Confidemus* (We Trust)
8. *Superbia in Proelio* (Pride in Battle)
9. *Victoria Concordia Crescit* (Victory Through Harmony)
10. *Floreat Salopia* (May Shropshire Flourish)

Arsenal
Bury
Kilmarnock
Sheffield Wednesday
Sunderland
Tottenham Hotspur
Everton
Shrewsbury
Blackburn
Manchester City

MATCH THE STADIUM TO THE CLUB

1. Camp Nou	Marseille
2. Estadio Santiago Bernabeu	Benfica
3. Signal Iduna Park	Bayer Leverkusen
4. San Siro	Bayern Munich
5. Allianz Arena	Galatasaray
6. Stadio Olimpico	Porto
7. Metropolitano Stadium	Paris Saint-Germain
8. Stade Vélodrome	Valencia
9. Estádio da Luz	Real Madrid
10. Johan Cryuff Arena	Barcelona
11. Stadio Diego Armando Maradona	Napoli
12. La Bombonera	FC Shakhtar Donetsk
13. Estádio do Dragão	Roma/Lazio
14. Mestalla Stadium	Ajax
15. Red Bull Arena	Red Star Belgrade
16. Türk Telekom Stadium	AC Milan/Inter
17. NSC Olimpiyskiy	Boca Juniors
18. Rajko Mitić Stadium	RB Leipzig
19. BayArena	Borussia Dortmund
20. Parc des Princes	Atlético Madrid

WOMEN'S FOOTBALL

1. Which England right back became the first woman to win the UEFA Women's Player of the Year Award in 2019?
2. Who did England lose to in the semi-finals of the Women's World Cup in 2019?
3. Who won the Ballon D'Or Féminin in 2019?
4. Who managed the England women's team from 2018 to 2021?
5. Which legend of the women's game won the FIFA World Player of the Year for five consecutive years between 2006 and 2010?

6. The USA have won the Women's World Cup how many times?
7. Which football star became the first woman to appear on the American cover of the video game *FIFA 16*, standing alongside Lionel Messi?
8. Which is the most successful club in the history of the UEFA Women's Champions League?
9. Which former England right back who notched up 140 caps for her country became a pundit in 2019?
10. Which player, now the England captain, became the first woman to appear on the cover of *Shoot* magazine in 2004?

SIX OF THE BEST ONE-CLUB FOOTBALLERS

1. Which Man Utd legend spent his entire career there, spanning 963 appearances?
2. Which Roma legend became the oldest goalscorer in the Champions League in 2014 aged 38 years and 59 days?
3. Which AC Milan legend spent 25 years there, winning 25 trophies and retiring at the age of 41 in 2009?
4. Which 1966 World Cup winner and later Republic of Ireland manager chalked up 762 appearances for Leeds United?
5. Which Barcelona central defender was captain from 2004 until he retired in 2014?
6. Which Chelsea legend became the first player to captain a side to the Premier League title five times?

MULTI-CLUB LEGENDS

These guys have been everywhere, yet they're legends at more than one club, so they're clearly doing something right!

1. James Milner has played for five different Premier League clubs. Can you get them all?
2. Emile Heskey has also played for five Premier League clubs. Can you name them?

3. Name Robbie Keane's six Premier League clubs, two of which were on loan
4. Peter Crouch has done one better, joining seven Premier League clubs. Name them!
5. Even Crouchy has to look up to someone, and in this case, it's Craig Bellamy, who became the first player to score for seven different Premier league clubs. Can you name them?

WORLD CUP

1. Which two players, one from England and one from Portugal, scored hat-tricks in the 1966 World Cup Finals?
2. Who was the youngest player to score a hat-trick at the World Cup Finals, which he did in the 1958 semi-final in a 5–2 victory over France?
3. Which Argentinian striker was the only player to score a hat-trick at the World Cup in 2010?
4. Which two players scored hat-tricks at the World Cup Finals in 2018?
5. The first match of the 2010 World Cup Finals was between Brazil and which team, making their second appearance since 1966?
6. Which player has made the most appearances at the World Cup Finals?
7. Who is the only player to score a hat-trick at two World Cups?
8. Which trio of countries is due to host the 2026 World Cup?
9. The 2010 World Cup is forever associated with which musical instrument?
10. Luis Suárez committed an infamous handball in the quarter-finals of the 2010 World Cup which he later called 'the save of the tournament'. Which country were Uruguay playing?
11. At the 2014 World Cup in Brazil, Luis Suárez bit which player on the shoulder?

12. England's first match at Italia 90 finished 1–1 with Gary Lineker scoring, but what else happened to Lineker during the game that he came clean about in 2010?
13. Who was denied a goal, which clearly crossed the line, in the last-16 stage against Germany at the 2010 World Cup?
14. Who tested positive for ephedrine during USA 94 and was expelled from the tournament?
15. Which striker handled the ball twice before crossing the ball to create a goal that booked France's place at the 2010 World Cup at the expense of Ireland?
16. Who was in goal when Maradona scored via the 'hand of God' in 1986?
17. Eleven different players have scored for England at the World Cup Finals across the last three tournaments (2010, 2014, 2018). Can you name them from the clues below?

    2010 England v United States: ______________________
    2010 Slovenia v England: ______________________
    2010 Germany v England: ______________________
    2014 England v Italy: ______________________
    2014 Uruguay v England: ______________________
    2018 Tunisia v England: ______________________
    2018 England v Panama: ______________________
    2018 England v Panama: ______________________
    2018 Sweden v England: ______________________
    2018 Sweden v England: ______________________
    2018 Croatia v England: ______________________

18. Three England players have been sent off at the World Cup. Who are they?
19. Two players have been sent off twice at the World Cup. One player managed this in 1998 and 2006, and the other was sent off in 1994 and 1998. Who are they?
20. Two Australian players were shown straight red cards in the group stages of the 2010 World Cup. Who are they?

EUROS

1. In which year was the first UEFA European Championship?
2. Which team knocked England out of the 1968 UEFA European Championship in the semi-final?
3. Which Dutch legend was the top scorer at Euro 1988?
4. Which player scored the most goals (nine) at a UEFA European Championship, a feat he achieved in 1984?
5. Which team did Germany beat to win Euro 96?
6. Who was the top scorer at Euro 96?
7. A record four English players appeared in the Euro 96 'Team of the Tournament'. Who were they?
8. Which country is the only one to win back-to-back European Championships?
9. Ahead of Euro 2016, UEFA announced their All-time Euro XI. Can you name the players from their nicknames/clues?

   Goalkeeper: Gigi
   Defender: Il Capitano (The Captain)
   Defender: Der Kaiser (The Emperor)
   Defender: El Tiburon (The Shark) aka Lionheart, Tarzan
   Defender: Most-capped German defender of all time
   Midfielder: El Cerebro (The Brain) aka El Ilusionista (The Illusionist)
   Midfielder: L'architetto (The Architect) aka Maestro, Mozart
   Midfielder: Zizou
   Forward: Five-time Ballon d'Or Winner
   Forward: Titi
   Forward: San Marco

10. Which French forward won both player of the tournament and the trophy for top scorer at Euro 2016?
11. Which two Welsh players appeared in the Euro 2016 'Team of the Tournament'?
12. Four England players scored at Euro 2016. Can you name them all?
13. Can you name all 24 teams that competed in Euro 2020?

14. Which two players shared the top scorer trophy at Euro 2020, with five goals each?
15. Which Chelsea player was awarded man of the match in Scotland's draw with England at Euro 2020?
16. Which Austrian forward and former Stoke City and West Ham player received a one-match ban for insulting another player against North Macedonia?
17. During a press conference in advance of Portugal's first group game at Euro 2020, Cristiano Ronaldo removed bottles of which drink from the table in front of him?
18. The FA was fined after a laser pointer was directed at the face of which Danish player during England's match against Denmark in the semi-final?
19. Italy's victory in the Euro 2020 final meant that they had now gone unbeaten in how many games?
20. Six of England's players appeared in every one of England's seven games. Can you name them?
21. Only three outfield players in England's 26-man squad did not play in the tournament. Can you name them?
22. Which England player was announced as going to join Manchester Utd from Borussia Dortmund during Euro 2020?
23. Only three teenagers have made the England starting line-up for a knockout game at a major men's football tournament. The first was at the World Cup in 1998, the second at Euro 2004 and the third at Euro 2020. Name them!
24. UEFA approved the use of how many substitutes during 90-minute matches at Euro 2020?
25. Which member of England's Euro 2020 squad plays their club football for Atlético Madrid as at July 2021?
26. Who scored their first senior international goal during England's Euro 2020 quarter-final match against Ukraine?
27. Gianluigi Donnarumma became only the second goalkeeper to win player of the tournament at a UEFA European Championship in 2021. Who was the other?

CHAMPIONS LEAGUE AND EUROPEAN CUP

1. Which English club won the European Cup in 1982?
2. Only five teams not belonging to the Spanish, Italian, German, English, French or Dutch leagues have won the European Cup. Which teams are they?
3. Which is the only team to have won five European Cups in a row?
4. English teams were the losing Champions League finalists for four successive years between 2006 and 2009. Name those clubs.
5. Who is the youngest coach to win the Champions League?
6. Liverpool's legendary comeback in the 2005 Champions League final occurred in which city?
7. Eleven English clubs have competed in the Champions League (including qualifying rounds) since it was rebranded in 1992. Name them.
8. Who is the only manager to win the Champions League, World Cup and European Championships?
9. Six English players have scored in a Champions League final. Name them!

ALL-TIME CHAMPIONS LEAGUE/EUROPEAN CUP SCORERS

Fill in the gaps in the table below:

Rank	Player	Nationality	Goals	Years	Club(s) (Goals)
1			134	2003–	________ (15) Real Madrid (105) ________ (14)
2			120	2005–	Barcelona
3		Polish	73	2011–	Borussia Dortmund (17) ________ (56)
4=	Raúl		71	1995–2011	________ (66) Schalke 04 (5)
4=		French	71	2006–	Lyon (12) Real Madrid (59)
6		Dutch	56	1998–2009	________ (8) Manchester United (35) ________ (13)
7			50	1997–2012	Monaco (7) Arsenal (35) ________ (8)
8		Argentinian	49	1955–1964	Real Madrid

UEFA CUP/EUROPA LEAGUE

1. Villareal beat Manchester United in the 2020/21 Europa League final after an extraordinary penalty shoot-out. How many penalties did Villareal score?
2. Which club has won the UEFA Cup/Europa League the most times?
3. Which team did Chelsea beat to win the 2019 Europa League?
4. Which English club, currently competing in League One, won the UEFA Cup in 1981 under the management of Sir Bobby Robson?

5. Which player has scored the most goals in the UEFA Cup/ Europa League, the vast majority of which he scored for Celtic?
6. Which team won the first UEFA Cup final, back in 1972, beating Wolverhampton Wanderers over two legs?
7. Since the final became a single match in 1998 rather than two legs, only three English players have scored in the final. Who are they?

_________ _________ (Liverpool v Alavés in 2001)
_________ _________ (Liverpool v Alavés in 2001)
_________ _________ (Liverpool v Sevilla in 2016)

FA CUP

1. Who was the first goalkeeper to save a penalty in the FA Cup final?
2. Which manager has won the most FA Cups?
3. Which player has won the most FA Cup winner's medals, winning three for Arsenal and four for Chelsea?
4. Which side beat Man City in the 2013 final?
5. Which Fourth Division team beat Arsenal in the third round in 1992?
6. Which two players combined at Highbury to score a hugely controversial winning goal against Sheffield United in the fifth round in 1999 that led Arsène Wenger to offer the Blades a replay?
7. Who scored a thunderous 35-yard half-volley to make the score 3–3 in the 91st minute of the 2006 final?
8. Which England legend, then aged 38, won his first FA Cup medal after producing the performance of his career to help his side win the 1953 final?
9. Which six players have been sent off in a FA Cup final?

ENGLISH LEAGUE CUP

1. From 1985 to today, the English League Cup has been known by eight different names due to the sponsorship deals it has attracted. Can you get all of them?

   1982–86: ______________________________
   1987–90: ______________________________
   1991–92: ______________________________
   1993–98: ______________________________
   1999–2003: ____________________________
   2004–12: ______________________________
   2013–16: ______________________________
   2019–present: __________________________

2. Four players have won the English League Cup four times. The first is Liverpool legend Ian Rush. The other three are all Man City players who won the tournament in 2014, 2016, 2018, 2019 and 2020. Who are they?

SERIE A

1. Which Italian club is known as *La Vecchia Signora* (The Old Lady)?
2. Can you match up the eight Serie A clubs with their colourful nicknames?

Rossoneri	Juventus
Nerazzurri	Napoli
Bianconeri	Parma
Viola	Lazio
Giallorossi	Inter
Azzurri	Roma
Gialloblu	AC Milan
Biancocelesti	Fiorentina

3. Which Italian club did David Platt join from Aston Villa in 1991?

4. Which Italian club did Paul Gascoigne join from Tottenham in 1992?
5. Which Italian club did Paul Ince join from Man Utd in 1995?

LA LIGA

1. Only three La Liga clubs have remained in the top flight since the league's inception in 1929. Two you'll get straight away, but which is the third club, who last won the league in 1984?
2. Aside from Barcelona, Real Madrid and Atlético Madrid, who was the last La Liga team to win the title?
3. Which Spanish club holds the record for most UEFA Cup/ Europa League wins?
4. Which player holds the record for most assists in La Liga?
5. In 1999–2000, which Spanish club won their first and only La Liga title to date?
6. Which Argentine-born forward and Real Madrid legend became a Spanish citizen in 1956?
7. As at 1 April 2021, who has made the most appearances at El Clásico?

GALÁCTICOS

Florentino Pérez's tenure as president of Real Madrid between 2000 and 2007 is known for his recruitment of football superstars, who became known as the Galácticos. Can you work out which legends are being described below?

1. Which player caused huge controversy by signing for Real Madrid in 2000 for €60 million from their arch rivals, becoming the first of the Galácticos?
2. Which 1998 Ballon d'Or winner smashed the world transfer record in 2001 by joining Real Madrid from Juventus?

3. Who joined Real Madrid from Inter Milan for approximately €45 million in 2002, the same year that he won the Golden Boot at the World Cup?
4. Which midfielder became a Galáctico in 2003 just four months after a notorious dressing room incident involving a flying boot that left him needing stitches?
5. Which Ballon d'Or winning English striker joined Real in 2004 but returned to the Premier League the following season?
6. Which Brazilian forward joined Real Madrid from Santos in 2005 before signing for Manchester City in 2008?
7. Which defender, who would go on to become Spain's most capped player, signed for Real in 2005 for €27 million from Sevilla?

USA, USA!

1. Which two USA players, both of whom played in the Premier League, share the record of most goals scored for their national team?
2. David Beckham became a co-owner of which MLS team, which launched in the 2020 season?
3. Which MLS club did Thierry Henry join from Barcelona in 2010?
4. Who helped Atlético Madrid win La Liga in 2014 before leaving to join the MLS?
5. In which stadium was the USA 94 World Cup Final held?
6. England and the USA played each other in the group stages of the World Cup in 2010, but what was the score?
7. Who managed the USA national team at the 2014 World Cup, navigating them through a difficult group and into the last 16?

DERBIES

1. Der Klassiker (The Classic) involves which two Bundesliga clubs?
2. The Derby della Capitale features which two Serie A clubs?
3. El Clásico is played between which two Spanish clubs?
4. Clássico is the name of the derby between which two Portuguese clubs?
5. The Paulista derby is played between which two Brazilian clubs?
6. De Klassieker is played between which two Dutch clubs?
7. The Intercontinental Derby features which two Turkish clubs?
8. The Superclásico takes place between which two Argentinian arch rivals?

FORMERLY KNOWN AS

Link up the current club name with its former name:

1. Dial Square	Wolverhampton Wanderers
2. Small Heath Alliance	Manchester City
3. St Luke's	Birmingham City
4. St Domingo	West Ham United
5. Newton Heath Lancashire and Yorkshire Railway	Everton
6. Thames Ironworks	Manchester United
7. St Mark's (West Gorton)	Arsenal

ANAGRAMS

Sort it out, son! Work out the names of these England captains.

1. BE BOY BROOM
2. AKIN KNEE VEG
3. LEAKY RINGER
4. ARSENAL HARE
5. DARTS REVENGER
6. NARKY RHEA
7. MONDAYS TA
8. ABSORB RONNY
9. INFRARED ODIN
10. CAPTURE STARE

Unscramble the names of these football grounds:

1. FAN IDLE
2. RUTH SPARKLES
3. FAT FORD LORD
4. RECONTACT VEGA
5. LADDER LOAN
6. DROOPING OAKS
7. SHEATH THROWN
8. GAMBITS REDFORD
9. FUR MOTOR
10. LEO UNMIX
11. BLUR HIGH LOOS
12. OAK POWDER
13. BELLMAN LARA
14. COWARD ROAR
15. HOGAN TEATS

Tricky away leg – find these jumbled up Bundesliga clubs:

1. BUN MACHINERY
2. TROUBADOURS MINDS
3. GLIB PRIZE
4. THANK CURRENT TARIFF
5. REVERSELY UNBAKE
6. ALAMO BUNCHING CHESSBOARD
7. BRETHREN HAIL
8. BUTT GRAFTS TV
9. BREWER MENDER
10. CUBS FUR GAG

COMMENTARY GOLD

Match the legendary quote to the commentator/presenter:

1. 'The Crazy Gang have beaten the culture club!'
2. 'Football is a simple game; 22 men chase a ball for 90 minutes and at the end, the Germans win.'
3. 'You can't win anything with kids.'
4. 'And Solskjaer has won it!'
5. 'Agueroooooooooooooo!!!! I swear you'll never see anything like this ever again!'
6. 'DENNIS BERGKAMP, DENNIS BERGKAMP, DENNIS BERGKAMP, DENNIS BERGKAMP, DENNIS BERGKAMP!!!!!!!!!!!'
7. 'Pelé! What a save! Gordon Banks!'
8. 'Oh, you beauty! What a hit, son. What a hit!'
9. 'And you have to say that is magnificent!'
10. 'The Dutch weren't ready, the defence wasn't steady, and there was good old Teddy!'

Clive Tyldesley
Martin Tyler
John Motson
Gary Lineker
Barry Davies
Andy Gray
Jonathan Pearce
Alan Hansen
Jack van Gelder
David Coleman

TRIVIA

1. In which year did Roman Abramovich take over Chelsea from Ken Bates?
2. In which year did Malcolm Glazer complete his takeover of Man Utd?
3. George Best made history in 1970 in the semi-final of the Watney Cup by becoming the first player to do what?
4. In the 1989–90 First Division, London had eight entrants in the top flight. Who were they?

5. Who took over from acting FIFA President Issa Hayatou in February 2016?
6. Which is the lowest ranked FIFA international men's team as at 1 July 2021?
7. Who was the last footballer to win BBC Sports Personality of the Year?
8. What is the name of the body that meets after games to adjudicate when it's not immediately clear who scored a goal?
9. FA President Prince William supports which club?
10. Which Sheffield United fan and *Fellowship of the Ring* actor has a tattoo that reads '100% Blade'?
11. Which European club competition ran for 39 seasons with its final edition played in 1999?
12. Which European club competition was discontinued after the 2008 tournament, which was won by Braga?

EUROPEAN CULT HEROES

Inspired by talkSPORT's Trans Euro Express where presenter Danny Kelly discusses classic players, can you identify these European legends?

1. This Italian striker enjoyed highly successful spells at Parma and Lazio, before signing for Chelsea in 2003.
2. This Italian defensive midfielder had stints at Juventus, Parma and Lazio in the 1990s and early 2000s. He briefly joined Blackburn on loan in 2003 and was capped 60 times for Italy.
3. French attacking midfielder who started both the 1998 World Cup Final and Euro 2000 final, but I'm sure he'd agree that his highlight was joining Bolton in 2002.
4. Prolific Uruguayan forward who was Inter's leading goalscorer in the 1992–3 and 1993–4 seasons.
5. Sweden's best player in their third-place finish at the 1994 World Cup, this midfielder/forward spent five years at Parma before joining Leeds United in 1995.

6. Italian right midfielder who was affectionately nicknamed 'Popeye' on account of his bald head and wiry physique, he joined Crystal Palace in 1997.
7. German central midfielder who captained Bayern Munich to the Champions League title in 2001. He famously gave the finger to the German fans during a group game against South Korea at USA 1994.
8. Dutch winger who made his name at Ajax in the late 1980s before a successful spell at Nottingham Forest from 1994 to 1997.
9. This Colombian forward was sold by Parma to Newcastle United in 1996, and arrived at his new club during a snowstorm wearing a fur coat.
10. This Chilean legend netted 101 times for Real Madrid over 173 games between 1992 and 1996 and scored 34 goals in 69 games for his country.
11. This Danish playmaker was one of the few who dared move from Barcelona to Real Madrid, which he did in 1994.
12. The Golden Boot winner at USA 94, this Bulgarian legend formed a hugely successful strike partnership with Romário at Barcelona.
13. The 1991 Ballon d'Or winner's goalscoring ability helped Marseille win four league titles in a row between 1989 and 1992.
14. One of the most influential number 10s of his era, this Portuguese attacking midfielder began and ended his career at Benfica, but became a Fiorentina legend in the 1990s.
15. French box-to-box midfielder turned Premier League manager, this player was a vital part of France's Euro 1984 victory.

BLASTS FROM THE PAST

1. Which speedy winger joined Man Utd from Shakhtar Donetsk for £650,000 in March 1991?
2. Which Middlesbrough legend joined them three times, in 1995, 1999 (on loan) and finally in 2002?
3. Who joined Leeds United in January 1995 and won Goal of the Season and the club's Player of the Year award the following season?
4. Which Bolton legend joined on a free transfer from Paris Saint-Germain in 2002 and soon became the subject of the chant 'So good, they named him twice.'
5. Who captained Blackburn's title-winning side of 1995?
6. Which tough-tackling defender was voted West Ham's Player of the Year four times between 1990 and 1997?

STANDS

Can you name the club from the names of the stands at its ground?

1. Whitehorse Lane Stand, Holmesdale Road, Main Stand, Arthur Wait Stand
2. Johnny Haynes Stand, Riverside Stand, Hammersmith End, Putney End
3. North Stand, South Stand, East Stand, Colin Bell Stand
4. Leazes Stand, Gallowgate Stand, East Stand, Milburn Stand
5. Northam Stand, Chapel Stand, Itchen Stand, Kingsland Stand
6. North Bank, Clock End, West Stand, East Stand
7. North Stand, Lisbon Lions Stand, Jock Stein Stand, Main Stand
8. Holte End, Trinity Road Stand, North Stand, Doug Ellis Stand
9. Brian Clough Stand, Bridgford Stand, Peter Taylor Stand, Trent End

10. Bill Shankly Kop, Invincibles Pavilion, Alan Kelly Town End, Sir Tom Finney Stand
11. Bill Struth Main Stand, Broomloan Road Stand, Sandy Jardine Stand, Copland Road Stand

CLOSEST GROUNDS

1. With their grounds – Dens Park and Tannadice Park – situated just 100 yards apart, which two Scottish clubs are the closest to each other?
2. Which two clubs, now in the Championship and Conference Premier respectively but formerly both members of the top flight, have grounds that are approximately 0.5 miles walking-distance apart?
3. Which two Premier League clubs' grounds are the closest, at approximately 0.7 miles walking-distance apart?
4. Which two Midlands clubs are separated by a walking distance of just over 3 miles?
5. Which two Yorkshire clubs are just over 3.5 miles apart?
6. To the nearest mile, how many miles are the Emirates and Tottenham Hotspur Stadium apart?
7. To the nearest mile, how close are Old Trafford and the City of Manchester (Etihad) Stadium?

BOXING

(ANSWERS PAGE 233)

talkSPORT has broadcast some of the biggest fights of the last decade as well as running the weekly Fight Night Show with Adam Caterall. So get your gloves on and hopefully you'll smash these questions.

BOXING (EASY)

MUHAMMAD ALI

1. Muhammad Ali changed his name from what?
   A: Darius Day **B:** Cassius Clay **C:** Theseus Ray
2. What was Muhammad Ali's nickname?
   A: The Best **B:** The Greatest **C:** Supreme
3. Which war did Muhammad Ali oppose on religious and ethical grounds?
   A: Second World War **B:** Cold War **C:** Vietnam War
4. Which weight division did Muhammad Ali compete in during his professional boxing career?
   A: Heavyweight **B:** Bantamweight **C:** Welterweight
5. Complete the famous Ali saying: 'Float like a butterfly …'
   A: Sting like a scorpion' **B:** 'Sting like a bee'
   C: 'Sting like a wasp'
6. Which UK talk show did Ali appear on four times between 1971 and 1981?
   A: *Wogan* **B:** *Parkinson* **C:** *Des O'Connor Tonight*
7. Which actor played Muhammad Ali in the 2001 film *Ali*?
   A: Will Smith **B:** Denzel Washington **C:** Morgan Freeman

ANTHONY JOSHUA

1. Anthony Joshua won gold at which Olympics representing Great Britain?
   A: Athens 2004 **B:** Beijing 2008 **C:** London 2012

2. Who did Anthony Joshua defeat in 2017 to claim the vacant WBA (Super) title?
A: Wladimir Klitschko **B:** Tyson Fury **C:** Lennox Lewis

3. What is Anthony Joshua's nickname?
A: Ant **B:** AJ **C:** A-JOSH

4. As of July 2021 how many fights has Anthony Joshua lost in his professional career?
A: 1 **B:** 3 **C:** 5

5. After a victory in 2017, who did Anthony Joshua call out in the post-fight interview with the line: _________, where you at baby? Come on – that's what they want to see.'
A: Kubrat Pulev **B:** Andy Ruiz Jr. **C:** Tyson Fury

6. In 2018, Anthony Joshua was awarded which honour by Prince Charles?
A: A knighthood **B:** An OBE **C:** The Booker Prize

7. Anthony Joshua has fought most of his professional fights in which city?
A: London **B:** Tokyo **C:** Dubai

TRIVIA

1. A boxing match typically takes place in an arena known as what?
A: A ring **B:** A square **C:** A pitch

2. The generally accepted rules in boxing are named after which British peer?
A: The Marquess of Queensbury **B:** The Count of Gunnersburyl **C:** The Viscount of Kingsbury

3. What is the correct name for a type of punch?
A: Hook **B:** Pull **C:** Scoop

4. Boxers are prohibited from hitting below which area?
A: The shorts **B:** The belt **C:** The breastbone

5. What are left-handed fighters nicknamed?
A: Westglove **B:** Northclub **C:** Southpaw

6. What can a boxer do to signify forfeiting or surrendering a match?
A: Throw down the gauntlet **B:** Throw in the towel
C: Throw a hat in the ring

7. Spot the fake weight class hiding among the real ones
A: Lightweight **B:** Heavyweight **C:** Superweight

8. A boxer who holds world titles from each of the four major sanctioning organisations is known as a what?
A: Unreal Champion **B:** Uncontested Champion
C: Undisputed Champion

9. Professional boxing bouts can last up to how many rounds?
A: 2 **B:** 4 **C:** 12

10. Complete the name of the two legendary boxing matches:
Rumble in the …
A: Tunnel **B:** Jungle **C:** Rubble

Thrilla in …
A: Manila **B:** Gibraltar **C:** Amarillo

BOXING (MEDIUM)

WHAT'S IN A NAME?

Match the most popular nicknames to the boxers:

1. Wladimir Klitschko	The Gypsy King
2. Vitali Klitschko	The Hit Man
3. Evander Holyfield	Smokin'
4. Mike Tyson	Dr Ironfist
5. Joe Frazier	Prince
6. Naseem Hamed	The Real Deal
7. Joe Louis	The Beast from the East
8. Floyd Mayweather	Iron
9. Tyson Fury	Dr Steelhammer
10. Deontay Wilder	Money
11. Manny Pacquiao	The Brown Bomber
12. Ricky Hatton	The Bronze Bomber
13. Nikolai Valuev	PacMan

EY, BIG FELLA

Can you place the following seven boxers in order of height from highest to lowest?

1. Lennox Lewis
2. Manny Pacquiao
3. Muhammad Ali
4. Floyd Mayweather Jr.
5. Nikolai Valuev
6. Tyson Fury
7. Mike Tyson

RECORD BREAKERS

1. Which boxer won BBC Sports Personality of the Year in both 1967 and 1970, becoming the first person to win the award twice?
2. Which featherweight boxer won SPOTY in 1985, becoming the first person not born in the UK to win the award?
3. Who became the first female boxer to win an Olympic Gold medal, a feat she accomplished at London 2012?
4. Who became the inaugural recipient of the SPOTY Lifetime Achievement Award in 1996, shortly after his retirement?
5. Who, aged 46, became the oldest man to win a boxing world championship, beating Jean Pascal by unanimous decision in 2011?
6. Which Welsh super-middleweight and light-heavyweight boxer retired in 2009 after an undefeated career?
7. Who, on his boxing debut, did Floyd Mayweather beat in August 2017 to take his undefeated record to 50–0?

TRIVIA

1. Who famously had part of their ear bitten off in a 1997 rematch with Mike Tyson?
2. Which boxing promoter said: 'I am the living attestation of the American dream. I am the extolment of this great nation'?
3. In a boxing ring, which two colours are the corners in which the two respective boxing teams are located?
4. Who triumphed over David Haye in their heavyweight unification fight in 2011?
5. How many seconds does a referee count to for a boxer to return to their feet after a knock down?
6. What is the name of the strategy that involves maintaining a defensive posture on the ropes to try and tire out his or her opponents?

7. What is the name of an illegal strike to the back of a fighter's head?
8. What does the abbreviation TKO stand for in boxing terminology?
9. Who competed in an exhibition boxing match in November 2020 against Roy Jones Jr., the bout ending in a draw?
10. World heavyweight champion from 1935–7, James J. Braddock, was known by which nickname that was inspired by a fairy tale?
11. Thirty-six boxing officials controversially involved in judging which Olympic Games were banned from the following Olympics?
12. What do the abbreviations WBA, WBC, WBO and IBF each stand for?
13. Which *Schindler's List* actor was crowned juvenile boxing champion of Northern Ireland in his youth?
14. Which heavyweight was outclassed by Tyson Fury in a rematch in February 2020 and lost his WBC title?

NAME THAT NATIONALITY

Which nationalities are the boxers below?

1. Vitali Klitschko ____________________
2. Nikolai Valuev ____________________
3. Manny Pacquiao ____________________
4. Juan Manuel Márquez ____________________
5. Katie Taylor ____________________

BOXING (HARD)

SIX OF THE BEST UPSETS

1. Who defeated WBC Champion Lennox Lewis with a second-round KO in September 1994 in London?
2. Which underdog defeated Marvin Hagler via a controversial split decision in April 1987 at Caesars Palace, Las Vegas, to claim the WBC middleweight title?
3. Which longshot beat Anthony Joshua by virtue of a technical KO in June 2019?
4. Which 42–1 longshot knocked out heavyweight champion Mike Tyson in February 1990 at the Tokyo Dome?
5. Who blew heavyweight champion Sonny Liston away in the sixth round causing him to throw in the towel before the seventh in February 1964 in Miami?
6. Who defeated Muhammad Ali in February 1978 via a 15th-round split decision at the Hilton in Las Vegas?

TRASH TALKING

Who spoke these immortal lines about their rivals in the run-up to their fights?

1. About Joe Frazier: 'Frazier's got two chances. Slim, and none. And Slim just left town.'
2. About Ricky Hatton: 'I'm going to punch him in his beer belly. He ain't good enough to be my sparring partner.'
3. About Lennox Lewis: 'I'm coming for you, man. My style is impetuous. My defense is impregnable, and I'm just ferocious. I want your heart. I want to eat his children. Praise be to Allah!'

4. About Vitali Klitschko: 'If he wants the rematch, there's no problem with that. I'll bust up the other side of his face, too.'
5. About Nikolai Valuev: 'He makes the elephant man look like Pamela Anderson.'
6. About Nigel Benn: 'Sure, he's educated to a certain extent, but under different circumstances he would be a bouncer on some door in the West End and he'd have three kids from three different women. I am a superior person to that.'
7. About Deontay Wilder: 'When I was training like a dosser, you couldn't keep me down then. You definitely can't keep me down now.'

TRIVIA

1. Who is the only heavyweight champion to finish his career undefeated?
2. Muhammad Ali famously lit the Olympic flame at Atlanta in which year?
3. Who is the only boxer to have received a knighthood?
4. Which boxer was the first African-American to become world heavyweight champion, a feat he managed in 1908?
5. Who is the only champion to win major world titles in eight different weight divisions?
6. Which light heavyweight became the oldest champion in boxing history by beating Jean Pascal via a unanimous decision in 2011 aged 46 years old?
7. Who is the only fighter to have become undisputed heavyweight champion on three separate occasions?
8. Which part of his body did David Haye break before his defeat to Wladimir Klitschko in 2011 which he claimed hampered his movement?
9. Which undisputed middleweight champion from 1980 to 1987 was known by the nickname 'Marvellous'?
10. In which Las Vegas hotel complex did Floyd Mayweather beat Ricky Hatton in 2007?

11. Which British boxer was caught arranging to supply a class A drug to the undercover reporter Mazher Mahmood, also known as the 'fake sheikh', in 2013?
12. Who became the first boxer to win titles from all four major sanctioning bodies (the WBA, IBF, WBC, and WBO), a feat he achieved in 1995 (winning the WBO portion)?
13. Which is the oldest of the four major sanctioning bodies in boxing?
14. Name the five boxers who have simultaneously held the WBA, WBC, WBO and IBF titles.

MATCH THE QUOTE WITH THE PERSON

1. 'Everybody has a plan until they get punched in the face.'
2. 'I hated every minute of training, but I said, "Don't quit. Suffer now and live the rest of your life as a champion."'
3. 'Boxing is the toughest and loneliest sport in the world.'
4. 'I remember as a little boy I ate one meal a day and sometimes slept in the street. I will never forget that, and it inspires me to fight hard, stay strong and remember all the people of my country, trying to achieve better for themselves.'
5. 'Why waltz with a guy for 10 rounds when you can knock him out in one?'
6. 'Sure the fight was fixed. I fixed it with my right hand.'
7. 'I think my greatest achievement in boxing is my following.'
8. 'I don't like to get hit, who likes it? I probably wouldn't do this sport if I was getting hit that much.'
9. 'Man, I hit him with punches that'd bring down the walls of a city.'

Frank Bruno
Rocky Marciano
Joe Frazier
Wladimir Klitschko
Muhammad Ali
Ricky Hatton
George Foreman
Manny Pacquiao
Mike Tyson

WEIGHT DIVISIONS

Can you put these nine weight divisions in the correct order from heaviest to lightest?

1. Bantamweight
2. Welterweight
3. Flyweight
4. Cruiserweight
5. Middleweight
6. Minimumweight
7. Featherweight
8. Heavyweight
9. Lightweight

BOXING AND HOLLYWOOD

1. Which two boxers appeared in the film *Ocean's Eleven* playing themselves?
2. Which fighter made a cameo appearance in the film *Rocky*?
3. Which boxing legend appears as a guest commentator in the 2010 film *The Fighter*?
4. Who was nominated for an Oscar for his portrayal of middleweight boxer Ruben 'Hurricane' Carter in 1999?
5. The film *Raging Bull*, which earned Robert De Niro an Oscar for Best Actor, is about the life of which boxer?
6. A tiger belonging to which former heavyweight champion goes missing in *The Hangover*?

WHERE IN THE WORLD?

1. The rematch between Anthony Joshua and Andy Ruiz Jr. in 2019 was controversially held in which country?
2. The famous 'Rumble in the Jungle' took place in which present-day African country?
3. In which city did Muhammad Ali and Joe Frazier fight in 1971?
4. The rematch between Dillian Whyte and Alexander Povetkin took place in which unusual location in March 2021?

5. Which boxer, who went on to become a unified cruiserweight world champion and WBA heavyweight champion, fought at the Playboy Mansion in 2003 against Vance Winn?
6. The third and final bout between Ali and Frazier for the heavyweight championship of the world took place in 1975 in which country?

FIRST-ROUND KOs

1. Against which then undefeated fighter did Mike Tyson complete a brutal 91-second knockout win in 1988?
2. Who knocked Sonny Liston out in the first round in a May 1965 rematch in controversial circumstances?
3. Which former WBO middleweight champion knocked out Reginaldo Dos Santos in 20 seconds at the Royal Albert Hall in 1990?
4. Who knocked out Said Lawal in 35 seconds to defend his WBO Featherweight title for the first time in 1996?
5. Which middleweight boxer, known as the 'Dark Destroyer', knocked out Ian Chantler in 1987 to extend his record to 10 knockouts in 10 fights?
6. Who knocked out heavyweight champion Floyd Patterson after two minutes and six seconds in September 1962 in Chicago in front of nearly 19,000 fans?

SPLIT DRAWS

1. Which two featherweights fighting for the WBA (Super) and IBF titles contested a hugely controversial split draw in May 2004 despite one of the fighters being knocked down three times in the first round?
2. Which two boxers, fighting to become undisputed heavyweight champion of the world, fought out a contentious split draw in March 1999 in Madison Square Garden?

3. In June 1989, which two super middleweight world champions met again, eight years after their first bout, and contested a split draw?
4. Which two heavyweights, with the WBC heavyweight title on the line, fought out a split draw in December 2018, remembered for its remarkable 'back from the dead' moment in the final round?
5. After an exhilarating final round, the bout between which two super middleweight Brits for the WBC and WBO titles ended in a split draw in October 1993?

GOING FOR GOLD

Can you match the champions to the year that they won Olympic gold?

1. Lennox Lewis (super heavyweight)
2. George Foreman (heavyweight)
3. James DeGale (middleweight)
4. Anthony Joshua (super heavyweight)
5. Wladimir Klitschko (super heavyweight)
6. Audley Harrison (super heavyweight)
7. Joe Frazier (heavyweight)
8. Oscar de la Hoya (lightweight)
9. Floyd Patterson (middleweight)
10. Cassius Clay (light heavyweight)

Helsinki 1952
Rome 1960
Tokyo 1964
Mexico City 1968
Seoul 1988
Barcelona 1992
Atlanta 1996
Sydney 2000
Beijing 2008
London 2012

CRICKET

(ANSWERS PAGE 240)

Did you know that talkSPORT presenter Darren Gough took a hat-trick against the Aussies in 1999 … in Sydney! It was the first by an Englishman in an Ashes series for almost 100 years. Get your pads on and see if you can navigate the corridor of uncertainty or get caught out by some of these teasers.

CRICKET (EASY)

TRIVIA

1. How many players are there in a cricket team?
   A: 9 **B:** 11 **C:** 15

2. What is the name of the Test cricket series played between England and Australia that takes place every other year?
   A: The Ashes **B:** The Embers **C:** The Cinders

3. Which ground is considered the home of cricket?
   A: Headingley **B:** Lord's **C:** Edgbaston

4. Which team won the last Cricket World Cup, in 2019?
   A: Australia **B:** New Zealand **C:** England

5. How many umpires are traditionally on the field of play during a cricket match?
   A: One **B:** Two **C:** Five

6. An 'over' consists of how many consecutive legal balls?
   A: Two **B:** Four **C:** Six

7. 'Dickie' Bird was a famous what?
   A: Cricket coach **B:** Umpire **C:** Mascot

8. Shane Warne played for which country?
   A: South Africa **B:** New Zealand **C:** Australia

9. Which cricketer won the BBC Sports Personality of the Year Award in 2019?
   A: Ben Stokes **B:** Joe Root **C:** Andrew Flintoff

10. What is the maximum number of overs that are bowled in a Twenty20 match?
A: 40 **B:** 80 **C:** 120

11. What is the maximum number of overs that are bowled in a one-day match?
A: 50 **B:** 100 **C:** 250

12. Which of the following is the correctly named international cricket team?
A: West Indies **B:** North Indies **C:** East Indies

13. Which ex-cricketer won the second series of *I'm a Celebrity … Get Me Out of Here!*?
A: Ashley Giles **B:** Phil Tufnell **C:** David Gower

CRICKETING TERMS AND ABBREVIATIONS

1. The 'baggy green' is a cap worn by cricketers playing for which country?
A: England **B:** India **C:** Australia

2. The term 'yorker' is used to describe a ball bowled in which area?
A: Around the batsman's feet **B:** At the batsman's head
C: At the batsman's privates

3. What is the name of an over in which no runs are scored by the batsmen?
A: Lady **B:** Maiden **C:** Spinster

4. What is the name given to the area outside a batsman's off stump, where the batsman has difficulty knowing whether or not to hit the ball?
A: The corridor of uncertainty **B:** The hallway of indecision
C: The atrium of unsureness

5. What is the collective name for the last and usually less skilful batsmen in a team?
A: Tail enders **B:** The dregs **C:** Wafters

6. What does LBW stand for?
A: Leg before wicket **B:** Lost behind wicket
C: Loose ball wide

7. What does NB stand for?
A: Not batting **B:** No ball **C:** Nasty ball

8. When a bowler appeals to an umpire for a decision about whether a batsman is out or not, what is the expression typically used?
A: Send him down! **B:** Howzat! **C:** Is he out?

9. A beamer is an expression used to describe a ball bowled at which height?
A: Around the head or upper body **B:** In the groin area
C: Over the batsman's head

10. What is the name for a ball that reaches the batsman without bouncing?
A: Quarter toss **B:** Half toss **C:** Full toss

11. What is the name of the stitching running around the circumference of a cricket ball?
A: Ticker tape **B:** Seam **C:** Hem

EQUIPMENT

1. How many stumps are there in a wicket?
A: One **B:** Two **C:** Three

2. What is the name of the small pieces of wood that rest on the top of the stumps?
A: Gates **B:** Willows **C:** Bails

3. What's the name of the device that protects a gentleman's nether regions?
   A: Box **B:** Slip **C:** Cup

4. Which wood is traditionally used to make cricket bats?
   A: Oak **B:** Redwood **C:** Willow

5. Cricket clothing for Test matches is usually which colour?
   A: White **B:** Yellow **C:** Pink

6. The exterior of a cricket ball is made of what material?
   A: Concrete **B:** Leather **C:** Wood

FIELD OF PLAY

1. Which of the following is a made-up fielding position?
   A: Silly Mid-Off **B:** Silly Point **C:** Stupid Long Leg

2. Spot the real fielding position lurking among the made-up ones.
   A: Third Man **B:** Ninth Man **C:** Man Three

3. What is the name of the player who stands behind the wicket at the batting end?
   A: Wicket-keeper **B:** Backstop **C:** Receiver

4. How long is a cricket pitch?
   A: 2 yards **B:** 22 yards **C:** 222 yards

5. What is the correct name for a particular area of the cricket field?
   A: Cow corner **B:** Pig pasture **C:** Rooster roundabout

6. What is usually used to demarcate the boundary or perimeter of a cricket field?
   A: Rope **B:** Wooden step **C:** White line

7. How many runs are scored if a batsman hits the ball over the boundary of a cricket field without bouncing?
   A: Six **B:** Eight **C:** Ten

8. How many runs does a batsman score if he or she hits the ball, which passes the boundary after touching the ground?
A: Two **B:** Four **C:** Six

NICKNAMES

1. Which country's cricket team are nicknamed the Proteas?
A: England **B:** Ireland **C:** South Africa

2. Which player was famously nicknamed 'Freddie'?
A: Andrew Flintoff **B:** Shane Warne **C:** Brian Lara

3. Which player was affectionately nicknamed 'Beefy'?
A: Kevin Pietersen **B:** Ian Botham **C:** Geoffrey Boycott

4. What is the name for the organised group of travelling England cricket team supporters?
A: Three Lions Lads **B:** Barmy Army **C:** Cricket Chaps

5. What is the name for the organised group of travelling Australia cricket team supporters?
A: Fanatics **B:** Zealots **C:** Disciples

6. Which team are known as the Black Caps?
A: Australia **B:** South Africa **C:** New Zealand

STRICTLY CRICKET

1. Which ex-cricketer won the third series of *Strictly Come Dancing* together with dance partner Lilia Kopylova?
A: Ian Botham **B:** Viv Richards **C:** Darren Gough

2. Which ex-cricketer won the next series of *Strictly* in 2006 with partner Karen Hardy?
A: Andrew Flintoff **B:** Mark Ramprakash
C: Nasser Hussain

3. Which ex-cricketer turned commentator got to week 9 of *Strictly* in 2009 with Katya Virshilas?
   A: Kevin Pietersen **B:** Shane Warne **C:** Phil Tufnell

4. Which former England cricket captain also made it to week 9 of *Strictly*, this time in 2012 before being voted out with dance partner Natalie Lowe?
   A: Michael Vaughan **B:** Michael Atherton
   C: Graham Gooch

5. As of July 2021, who was the last former cricketer to appear on *Strictly*, going out in week 10 with partner Oti Mabuse?
   A: Alastair Cook **B:** Graeme Swann **C:** Geoffrey Boycott

TRUE OR FALSE

1. It is illegal to bowl the ball underarm unless a special agreement is made before the match between the two teams.
2. A Test match cannot end in a draw.
3. In a match played during the day, the umpires can take the players off the field because of 'bad light' if the ball has become difficult to see.
4. A googly is a term used to describe a particularly bumpy pitch.
5. A batsman who gets out on the first ball he or she faces is said to be out for a golden duck.
6. Australia has never won the Cricket World Cup.
7. Scotland won the last one-day match against England in 2018.
8. An umpire signals that a batsman is out by raising his or her index finger.
9. The word cricket derives from the French 'crickette' meaning 'hollow wood'.
10. A cricket ground must be a perfect circle.

CRICKET (MEDIUM)

THE T20 BLAST

Connect the county/city with the correct second part of its team name:

1. Derbyshire	Eagles
2. Lancashire	Sharks
3. Leicestershire	Falcons
4. Northants	Bears
5. Notts	Lightning
6. Birmingham	Spitfires
7. Worcestershire	Foxes
8. Yorkshire	Steelbacks
9. Essex	Rapids
10. Kent	Outlaws
11. Sussex	Vikings

INDIAN PREMIER LEAGUE TEAMS

Connect the place or area with the other part of its team name:

1. Chennai	Royal Challengers
2. Delhi	Kings
3. Kolkata	Royals
4. Mumbai	Super Kings
5. Punjab	Knight Riders
6. Rajasthan	Sunrisers
7. Bangalore	Capitals
8. Hyderabad	Indians

LINE-UPS

Can you fill in the missing letters to make up the England and Australia XIs from the famous second Test during the 2005 Ashes series, which England won by just two runs? (The first two letters of both the first name and surname of each player are provided to help you.)

England

1. Ma Tr
2. An St
3. Mi Va (c)
4. Ia Be
5. Ke Pi
6. An Fl
7. Ge Jo †
8. As Gi
9. Ma Ho
10. St Ha
11. Si Jo

Australia

1. Ju La
2. Ma Ha
3. Ri Po (c)
4. Da Ma
5. Mi Cl
6. Si Ka
7. Ad Gi †
8. Sh Wa
9. Br Le
10. Ja Gi
11. Mi Ka

† = wicket-keeper; (c) = captain

ANAGRAMS

Can you work out the members of the England XI who faced New Zealand in the 2019 World Cup Final from the anagrams below?

1. SONAR JOY
2. JINNY ROWBOATS
3. REO TOJO
4. ANNIE GROOM
5. BEES TONKS
6. BRUTE JOLTS
7. SOCK WASHIER
8. MULTIPLE TANK
9. FORCER JARAH
10. RADIAL DISH
11. WORD AMOK

LESSER-KNOWN CRICKET-PLAYING NATIONS

Aside from the 12 full members of the International Cricket Council, can you work out which other nations have competed at the Cricket World Cups from the clues below?

1. Home to the Maasai Mara.
2. England have only played two T20 matches against this Low Country and lost both.
3. Its national flag features a maple leaf.
4. Resigned from the UK Cricket Council in 1992 and was granted independent associate membership of the ICC in 1994.
5. Dubai and Abu Dhabi are two of the constituents of this country.
6. Sprinter Frankie Fredericks represented this southern African nation.
7. Known for a perilous region of sea that forms a geometric shape.

WHAT HAPPENED NEXT?

1. It's the first ball of the Ashes on 23 November 2006 at the Gabba and Steve Harmison runs in. What happens next?
2. It's the final over of the 2016 World T20 final and Ben Stokes is bowling to Carlos Brathwaite. The West Indies need 19 to win …
3. It's the final of the 2019 World Cup and England need nine to win from three balls. Ben Stokes lashes the ball down towards the leg-side boundary and comes back for a risky second run …
4. It's 24 March 2018 and South Africa are playing Australia in the third Test at Newlands with the series tied at 1–1. It's the 43rd over of South Africa's second innings and Cameron Bancroft receives the ball …

5. It's January 1999 and England are playing Sri Lanka in the Tri-Nation ODI Series in Adelaide. Muttiah Muralitharan is bowling the 18th over. What happens after he bowls his fourth ball?
6. It's February 1981 and Australia are playing New Zealand at the MCG. New Zealand need six to tie from the final ball to be bowled by Trevor Chappell. What happens next?
7. It's 4 June 1993 and Shane Warne steps up to bowl his first delivery against England in his first Ashes Test. The experienced Mike Gatting is the batsman. What happens next?

SLEDGING

Match the following players to their famous sledges below: Shane Warne, Andrew Flintoff, Merv Hughes, Viv Richards, Dennis Lilley, Darren Gough.

1. Who cautioned Tino Best to 'Mind the Windows' in 2004 as Best readied himself to send Ashley Giles into the pavilion, only to swing and miss, leaving Geraint Jones to stump him?
2. In a day–night match in 2005, who hilariously impersonated a ghost while walking past Shane Watson in reference to Watson reportedly having trouble sleeping at the allegedly haunted Lumley Castle where the Australians were staying?
3. Who said 'Good morning, Shermanator' to Ian Bell during the 2006 Ashes?
4. Who responded to Javed Miandad's jibe that he looked like a 'fat bus driver' with 'Tickets please!' after he took Miandad's wicket?
5. Who allegedly checked his run-up during an Ashes Test to say, 'Hey, Gatt, move out of the way. I can't see the stumps' to Mike Gatting?
6. Glamorgan fast bowler Greg Thomas once mockingly told who that '… it's red, it's round and it's fast. Now try playing it!' only to be smashed out of the ground the next ball, followed by the line: 'You know what it looks like, now you go and find it!'?

TROPHIES

Match the name of the trophy to the teams that contest it:

1. Warne–Muralitharan Trophy	South Africa–West Indies
2. Wisden Trophy	Australia–India
3. Freedom Trophy	Australia–West Indies
4. Border–Gavaskar Trophy	West Indies–Sri Lanka
5. Sir Vivian Richards Trophy	Australia–Sri Lanka
6. Frank Worrell Trophy	India–South Africa
7. Trans–Tasman Trophy	England–India
8. Basil D'Oliveira Trophy	England–West Indies
9. Pataudi Trophy	Australia–New Zealand
10. Sobers–Tissera Trophy	England–South Africa

RECORD-BREAKING BATSMEN

As of July 2021, only 13 batsmen have scored over 10,000 Test runs in their careers. Can you name them from the clues below?

Name	Runs	Country	Test Career Span
	15,921	India	1989–2013
	13,378	Australia	1995–2012
	13,289	South Africa	1995–2013
	13,288	India	1996–2012
	12,472	England	2006–2018
	12,400	Sri Lanka	2000–2015
	11,953	West Indies	1990–2006
	11,867	West Indies	1994–2015
	11,814	Sri Lanka	1997–2014
	11,174	Australia	1978–1994
	10,927	Australia	1985–2004
	10,122	India	1971–1987
	10,099	Pakistan	2000–2017

RECORD-BREAKING BOWLERS

As at 1 September 2021, only 16 bowlers in the history of Test cricket have taken over 400 wickets. Can you name them from their initials for their first name (or first name they are commonly known by) and last names? (★ = still playing)

Name	Country	Wickets
MM	Sri Lanka	800
SW	Australia	708
JA*	England	630
AK	India	619
GM	Australia	563
SB*	England	524
CW	West Indies	519
DS*	South Africa	439
KD	India	434
RH	Sri Lanka	433
RH	New Zealand	431
SP	South Africa	421
HS	India	417
WA	Pakistan	414
RA*	India	413
CA	West Indies	405

TOP TEST SCORES

Can you fill in the names of batsmen with the highest single-innings scores in the history of Test cricket from the clues below? (* = not out)

1.	400*	The Prince	
2.	380	Australian left-handed batsman who opened with Justin Langer	
3.	375	The Prince again!	
4.	374	Sri Lankan legend who retired from Test cricket in 2014	
5.	365*	One of the best all-rounders to play the game, he was made one of ten National Heroes of Barbados by act of Parliament in 1998	
6.	364	Yorkshire legend, former England captain and later Test selector and broadcaster	
7.	340	Sri Lankan all-rounder who hit a James Anderson over for six fours in his final Test innings	
8.	337	First Pakistani to score a triple hundred, which he did in 1958; also reached a record-breaking 499 for Karachi in 1959	
9.	336*	England captain before and after the Second World War	
10.	335*	Australian vice-captain from 2015 to 2018 but suspended from cricket for a year after the ball tampering scandal of 2018	
11=	334	Legend who finished his Test career with a scarcely believable average of 99.94	
11=	334*	Australian opening batsman and captain from 1994 to 1999	
13=	333	Essex legend, England opening batsman and captain from 1988 to 1993	
13=	333	West Indian big-hitter with the most sixes in international cricket, as at August 2021	

KNIGHTS OF THE REALM

A number of famous former cricketers have been knighted for services to cricket. Can you fill in the missing letters below to reveal their identities?

1. D_ _ B_ _ _ _an (Australia, knighted 1949)
2. _ _ c_a_d H _ _ _ee (New Zealand, knighted 1990)
3. _i_ _i_h_ _ds (West Indies, knighted 1999)
4. I_n _ _th_ _ (England, knighted 2007)
5. R_ _ _ie R_ _ _ _ _ _ _ _on (West Indies, 2014)
6. _ur_ _y _mbr_ _e (West Indies, 2014)
7. A_ _ _ _ _ir _ _ok (England, 2019)
8. G_ _ _ _ _ey B_yc_ _ _ (England, 2019)
9. _n_ _ew _ _rau_ _ (England, 2019)
10. _ _rdo_ Gr_ _ _ _ _ _e (West Indies, 2020)
11. Cl _ _ _ Ll_ _ _ (West Indies, 2020)

COUNTY LEGENDS

1. Joe Root and Michael Vaughan are associated with which English county team?
2. Andrew Flintoff and Michael Atherton played for which English county?
3. Which county did Graham Gooch captain for over 20 years?
4. Alec Stewart played for which county between 1981 and 2003?
5. Mike Gatting played for which county for the whole of his career?
6. Paul Collingwood played his entire domestic career for which county?
7. Graeme Hick played for which county between 1984 and 2008?
8. Which cricketing legend played for Gloucestershire between 1870 and 1899?

9. Viv Richards moved to Taunton in 1974 when he joined Somerset, but with which English player did he both share a flat and strike up an enduring friendship?

MATCH THE ENDS TO THE STADIUMS

1. Nursery End, Pavilion End
2. Birmingham End (previously City End), Pavilion End
3. James Anderson End, Brian Statham End
4. Radcliffe Road End, Pavilion End
5. River End, Marcus Trescothick Pavilion End
6. Lumley End, Finchale End
7. Vauxhall End, Pavilion End
8. River Taff End, Cathedral Road End
9. Ashley Down Road End, Bristol Pavilion End
10. Kirkstall Lane End, Football Stand End

The Oval
Trent Bridge
Bristol County Ground (Nevil Road)
Riverside Ground (Chester-le-Street)
Lord's
Edgbaston
Headingley
County Ground, Taunton
Old Trafford
Sophia Gardens

WHO ARE THEY ON ABOUT?

Which fast-bowling legends are being talked about below?

1. 'I have an awful lot of respect for ________. Good luck to him. I believe once he goes past me he will never be beaten.' Which record-breaking bowler is Glenn McGrath describing here?
2. 'I'm not sure if I'm looking forward to facing __________ again. He bowls at 95mph so enjoyment is not the word I would use.' Which Aussie quick bowler is Andrew Flintoff talking about here?

3. 'Let's be honest, __________ was a massive threat. You had Shaun Pollock, who would test your technique, but __________ would test your ticker and technique.' Which South African fast bowler kept Nasser Hussain on his toes?
4. 'He was probably the most skilled fast-bowler I played against and it wasn't just with the new ball either … He had an ability to swing the new ball both ways close to 150kph. And when the ball got old, the reverse swing skills he had were quite remarkable.' Which Pakistan legend is Ricky Ponting praising here?

TRIVIA

1. What do the letters MCC stand for?
2. Which legendary cricketer is now the prime minister of Pakistan as at August 2021?
3. What does the W and G stand for in W.G. Grace?
4. Who holds the record for the highest Test batting average?
5. Which two animals surround the shield on the Australian Cricket Coat of Arms?
6. Which team beat India by nine runs in the final of the Women's World Cup in 2017?
7. Brian Lara only played for one English county team. Which one was it?
8. Which former Manchester United and England defender is Andrew Flintoff describing on talkSPORT in 2020: 'I played junior cricket at Lancashire with __________. He was a year older than me and he was a cricketing genius.'
9. Which all-rounder nearly joined Crystal Palace Football Club as an apprentice in his teens?
10. Father Time is the name of the famous weathervane at which cricket ground?
11. The 2019 Cricket World Cup was held in England and which other nation?

12. Which England player was involved in a notorious incident involving a pedalo in 2007?

13. Which company issued the following statement in August 2019: 'We can confirm we will offer Jack Leach free glasses for life.'

14. Who won the Cricket World Cup in 2015, beating New Zealand by seven wickets?

15. Which former international captain was banned from cricket for life in 2000?

CRICKET (HARD)

HEAD AND SHOULDERS ABOVE THE REST

Can you match the following tallest players in cricket history to their respective heights below? Steven Finn, Joel Garner, Mitchell Starc, Glenn McGrath, Chris Tremlett, Jacob Oram, Shaheen Afridi, Curtly Ambrose, Bruce Reid, Mohammad Irfan, Jason Holder, Tony Grieg, Morné Morkel.

1.	7 ft 1 in	Pakistani left-arm fast bowler 2010–19	
2.	6 ft 8 in	West Indian right-arm fast bowler 1977–87	
3.	6 ft 8 in	Australian left-arm fast-medium bowler 1985–92	
4.	6 ft 7 in	English right-arm fast-medium bowler 2005–13	
5.	6 ft 7 in	West Indian right-arm fast bowler 1998–2000	
6.	6 ft 7 in	West Indian all-rounder 2013–	
7.	6 ft 7 in	English right-arm fast bowler 2010–17	
8.	6 ft 6 in	New Zealand right-arm fast-medium bowler 2001–12	
9.	6 ft 6 in	English all-rounder 1972–77	
10.	6 ft 6 in	Australian left-arm fast bowler 2010–	
11.	6 ft 6 in	Pakistani left-arm fast bowler 2018–	
12.	6 ft 6 in	Australian fast-medium bowler 1993–2007	
13.	6 ft 5 in	South African right-arm fast bowler 2006–18	

METHODS OF DISMISSAL

There are ten methods by which a batsman can be given out. Can you name them all?

1. ______________________
2. ______________________
3. ______________________
4. ______________________
5. ______________________
6. ______________________
7. ______________________
8. ______________________
9. ______________________
10. ______________________

FIELDING POSITIONS

Can you name all of the 32 fielding positions on the graphic below?

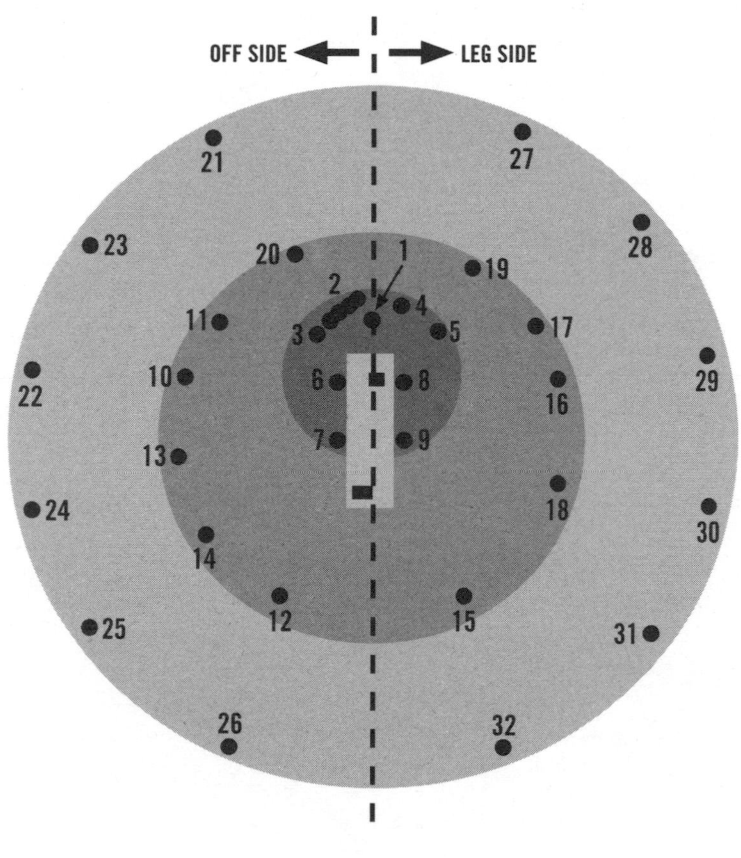

WHERE IN THE WORLD?

Match the names of these famous grounds to their locations on the world map:

Newlands, Cape Town
WACA, Perth
MCG, Melbourne
SCG, Sydney
Galle International

Wankhede Stadium, Mumbai
Eden Gardens, Kolkata
Eden Park, Auckland
Queen's Park Oval, Trinidad
National Stadium, Karachi
Gaddafi Stadium, Lahore
Wanderers Stadium (the Bullring), Johannesburg
Basin Reserve, Wellington

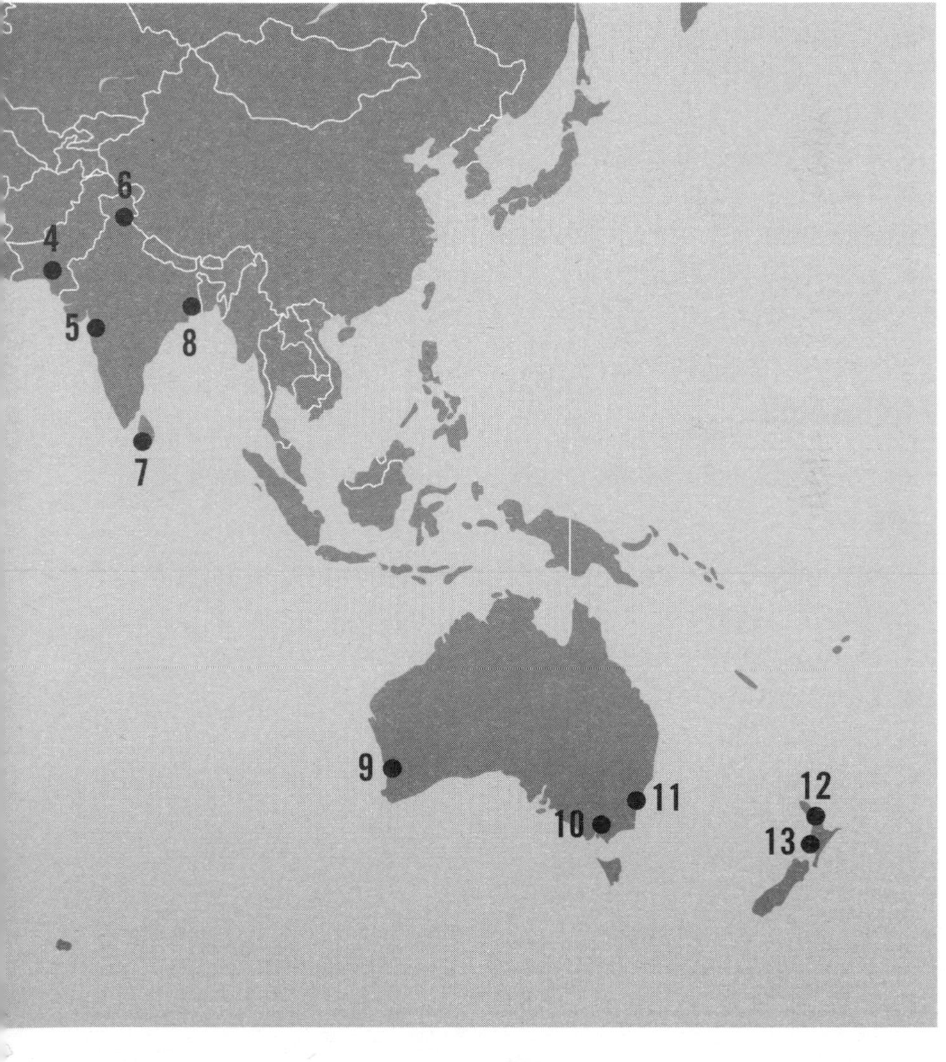

NICKNAMES

Cricketers come up with some of the finest mickey-taking nicknames around. Can you match the nickname with the player? See the answer pages for the story of how they came about.

1. Punter	Sachin Tendulkar
2. The Little Master	Glenn McGrath
3. Mr 360	Shoaib Akhtar
4. Beefy	Mike Hussey
5. Freddie	Alastair Cook
6. The Pigeon	Ricky Ponting
7. Chef	Andrew Flintoff
8. The Rawalpindi Express	AB de Villiers
9. The Cat	Phil Tufnell
10. The Wall	Ian Botham
11. The King of Spain	Rahul Dravid
12. Mr Cricket	Ashley Giles

ANAGRAMS

Can you work out the names of these jumbled-up England Test captains?

1. ALMANAC HIVE HUG
2. AMINO BATH
3. DOWN NAFF TRIFLE
4. OVERDID WAG
5. EERILY EMBARK
6. EASTWARDS RUNS
7. SAUNAS SHINERS
8. HARMONIC ATHLETE
9. ACHROMA GOGH
10. OREO JOT
11. RASCAL TWEET
12. GAME KITTING
13. BOWL IBLIS
14. COFFEE GROTTY YOB
15. CREW GAG

Can you unscramble the names of the all-time leading run scorers in Tests?

1. AUCKLAND HINTERS
2. CRYPT OINKING
3. JACKIE SQUALLS
4. CROATIA KOLAS
5. DAD HURL RIVA
6. ARGUS KANAKA MARK
7. BAR LARINA
8. ANNUAL CHIP REVARNISHED
9. DEJA RENEWAL YAMAHA
10. ANDORRA BELL

BUNNIES

Match the batsman to the bowler they were dismissed by the most:

1. Graham Gooch	Harbhajan Singh (10 dismissals)
2. Michael Atherton	Stuart Broad (12 dismissals)
3. Ian Healy	Courtney Walsh (15 dismissals)
4. Nasser Hussain	Malcolm Marshall (16 dismissals)
5. Mark Waugh	Curtly Ambrose (15 dismissals)
6. Greg Chappell	Derek Underwood (13 dismissals)
7. Allan Border	Shane Warne (11 dismissals)
8. Mark Boucher	Glenn McGrath (19 dismissals)
9. David Warner	Ian Botham (12 dismissals)
10. Ben Stokes	Ravichandran Ashwin (11 dismissals)
11. Sunil Gavaskar	Muttiah Muralitharan (12 dismissals)
12. Ricky Ponting	Derek Underwood (12 dismissals)

CRICKET-PLAYING COUNTIES

Here's a fiendishly tricky one. Can you list, using the map below, the 18 counties who play in Divisions One and Two of the County Championship?

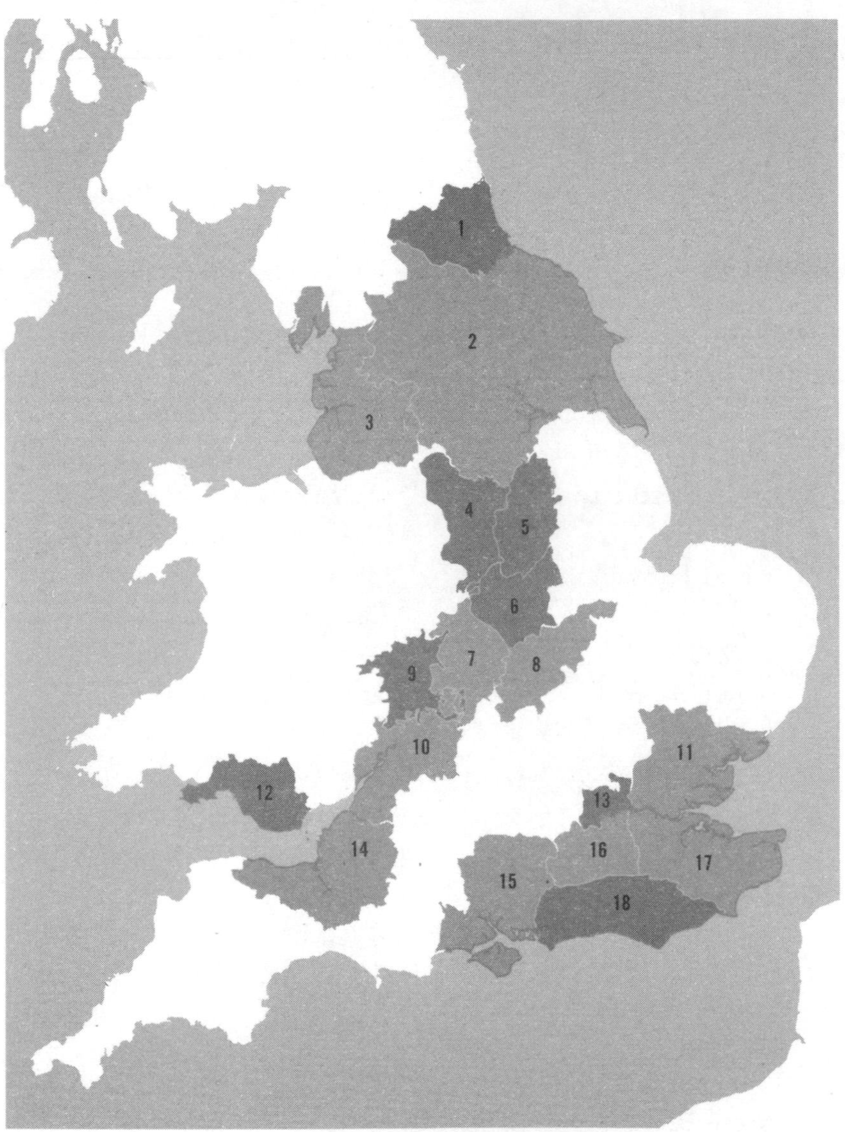

ALL TIME WORLD CUP XI

In 2021, *Wisden* announced their all-time World Cup XI. Can you guess them from the clues?

1. Indian batting legend whose international career spanned 1989–2013.
2. Indian batsman who broke the record for most centuries scored in a single World Cup in 2019 and won ICC ODI Player of the Year 2019.
3. Most successful Australian captain in terms of matches won in ODIs.
4. Sri Lankan batsman and wicket-keeper; won ICC Player of the Year in 2011 and 2013.
5. West Indian batsman whose international career spanned 1974–1991; selected in 2002 as the greatest ODI batsman of all time by *Wisden*.
6. Pioneering South African batsman and former captain who holds the record for fastest century in ODI cricket (31 balls).
7. South African all-rounder 1996–2004.
8. Legendary Pakistani left-arm fast bowler.
9. Australian left-arm fast bowler and World Cup winner 2015.
10. Australian great famous for line and length.
11. Highest Test wicket-taker of all time.

TRIVIA

1. In which country is the Kensington Oval situated?
2. Which umpire famously lifted one foot off the ground whenever the score reached 111 or multiples of it?
3. Who are the only two bowlers ever to have claimed ten wickets in a Test match innings?
4. Which former Sri Lankan player was appointed as the first non-British President of the MCC in 2019?

5. Which country posted a first-innings total of 952/6 in August 1997, breaking the previous record for runs scored in a single innings?
6. Which bowler, with a Test career spanning 2006–2013, holds the record for England's lowest batting average?
7. Which fellow bowler, whose Test career lasted from 1990 to 2001, did the answer to the previous question bump off 'top' spot for England's lowest batting average?
8. Who was dismissed for handling the ball after blocking a short delivery from Merv Hughes in 1993?
9. The hugely controversial practice of running out a batsman who is backing up is known by what name, after an incident during India's tour of Australia in 1947–8?
10. Which iconic feature of the St Lawrence Ground in Canterbury, Kent was lost after high winds in January 2005?
11. If the ball strikes a helmet placed on the field of play by the fielding team, how many penalty runs are awarded to the batting team?
12. In Twenty20 cricket, how long does the first powerplay last?
13. In 2017, Marnus Labuschagne was the first player to be penalised for which action after attempting to intercept a drive?
14. Which bizarre moment occurred when a delivery from Mushtaq Ahmed made its way towards Pat Symcox in a Test between Pakistan and South Africa in 1997?
15. Who became the most expensive acquisition in IPL history during the 2021 IPL auction?

MASTER BLASTERS

1. Which batsman held the record for highest individual Test score for six months before he was eclipsed by Brian Lara in April 2004?
2. Who holds the record for most total runs scored in a single Test match?

3. Who, on his Test debut in February 2021, scored an unbeaten 210 for the West Indies against Bangladesh to successfully chase down a target of 395?
4. Who holds the record for the highest individual score (264) recorded in a One-Day International?
5. Who set the record for the highest individual one-day score by an English batsman (180) in 2018 against South Africa?
6. Who blasted their way to a record-breaking 172 in a Twenty20 game against Zimbabwe in 2018?
7. Who only needed a record-breaking 16 balls to smash a 50 in an ODI against the West Indies in 2015?
8. Who only needed two overs to memorably club his way to 50 against England in 2007, setting the record for the fastest 50 in Twenty20 cricket?
9. Who became the youngest player to score a double hundred in Test cricket, at 19 years and 140 days, which he achieved for Pakistan in 1976 against New Zealand?
10. In 1958, which West Indian legend scored 365 not out in a Test match against Pakistan aged just 21?

DARTS

(ANSWERS PAGE 257)

We always hit the bullseye with our darts coverage on talkSPORT with award-nominated commentary by Ian Danter and co. In 2021 we became the exclusive broadcaster of the World Matchplay, and what a blinder that was. So step up to the oche and have a pop at this lot. Game on!

DARTS (EASY)

TRIVIA

1. What shape is a regular darts board?
   A: Circle **B:** Oval **C:** Rectangle

2. In darts, both players start with which score?
   A: 101 **B:** 501 **C:** 1,001

3. What is the highest score that can be achieved with three darts?
   A: 100 **B:** 140 **C:** 180

4. What is the lowest score someone can achieve with three scoring darts?
   A: 1 **B:** 3 **C:** 10

5. What is the name for the centre of a dartboard, comprising a red circle and a green outer ring?
   A: Bullseye **B:** Maximum C: Ten bob bit

6. A score of 'double top' is worth how many points?
   A: 5 **B:** 40 **C:** 75

7. The line behind which each player throws is called what?
   A: The ache **B:** The eche **C:** The oche

8. In darts, each player takes turns to throw how many darts?
   A: Two **B:** Three **C:** Four

9. Which one of the following is a famous former darts player?
   A: Erin Bristau **B:** Aaron Bristol **C:** Eric Bristow

10. Darts legend Phil Taylor is known by which nickname?
A: Phil 'The Power' Taylor **B:** Phil 'The Force' Taylor
C: Phil 'The Voltage' Taylor

DARTS (MEDIUM)

Can you add the 20 numbers around the outer edge of the dart board below?

NICKNAMES

Darts nicknames are legendary. See if you can match the nicknames of these current and former pros to the players:

1. Wolfie	Co Stompé
2. The Power	John Part
3. The Count	Gary Anderson
4. The Crafty Cockney	Phil Taylor
5. Jackpot	Peter Wright
6. The Flying Scotsman	John Lowe
7. Voltage	Ted Hankey
8. The Matchstick	Rob Cross
9. Old Stoneface	Eric Bristow
10. Snakebite	Martin Adams
11. Darth Maple	Adrian Lewis

TRIVIA

1. Which famous venue hosted the BDO World Championships from 1986 to 2019?
2. Which venue became the new host for the BDO World Championship in 2020?
3. Which venue became the new host for the PDC World Championship from 2008?
4. Who did Phil Taylor beat in three successive PDC World Championship finals between 1996 and 1998?
5. Professional darts players tend to use darts made with between 80 and 95% of which metal?
6. To the nearest 50mm, what is the diameter of a regulation dartboard?
7. Which famous darts player sponsored Phil Taylor with around £10,000 to help him establish himself in the game as a professional in the late 1980s?

DARTS (HARD)

TRIVIA

1. The PDC World Championship trophy was renamed in honour of which former commentator who passed away in 2012?
2. Who became the first player to throw a nine-darter at the PDC World Championship?
3. Which legend has won the BDO Women's World Championship ten times?
4. Who made history by becoming the first woman to beat a man in the PDC World Championship in 2019?
5. In which year was the World Darts Council formed before later renaming itself the Professional Darts Corporation (PDC)?
6. Only three players from outside the UK have won the PDC World Championship. Can you name them and the years they won?
7. In which year was the first Women's BDO World Championship held?
8. In which year did Phil Taylor finish second in BBC's Sports Personality of the Year?
9. The World Matchplay finals have, with one exception, all taken place at which northern venue?
10. Which sports promoter is the chairman of the PDC as at July 2021?

WALK-ON MUSIC

Walk-on music is all part of the great game of darts and says a lot about a player and their fans. But mostly, it's a wonderful excuse for a boozed-up crowd to have a singalong. We wouldn't have it any other way. Can you match the songs to the current and former players?

1. 'Eye of the Tiger' by Survivor
2. 'Seven Nation Army' by the White Stripes
3. 'Can't Touch This' by MC Hammer
4. 'The Imperial March' by John Williams
5. 'Cotton Eye Joe' by Rednex
6. 'The Power' by Snap
7. 'Don't Stop the Party' by Pitbull
8. 'Hungry Like the Wolf' by Duran Duran
9. 'Jump Around' by House of Pain

Phil Taylor
Peter Wright
Martin Adams
Gary Anderson
John Walton
John Part
Andy Hamilton
Raymond van Barneveld
Michael van Gerwen

ANAGRAMS

Can you unscramble the letters to reveal the famous current and former darts players?

1. CORR SOBS
2. JAN THORP
3. JAW SEAMED
4. APRIL HOTLY
5. BOGEY GOBBER
6. CLOWN JOYSKI
7. SORBIC WRITE
8. GIRTH PEWTER
9. CREWING PREY
10. PINKIE TAVERN
11. GRUNT LANDER
12. SALARIED WIN
13. DRAGONS YEARN
14. ABNORMAL DANNY REVVED
15. CHINA ENGRAVE MEWL

F1

(ANSWERS PAGE 262)

Take your positions on the starting grid for this section and we'll see if you know your DRS from your downforce or your Fangio from your Fittipaldi. As ever, we've got some easy ones to start with but they're followed by a few that will stretch your tyres to the max. Or are you just all torque?

F1 (EASY)

TRIVIA

1. What colour is the flag waved at the finishing line?
   A: Green **B:** Chequered black and white
   C: Red and yellow

2. What does 'SC' stand for in Formula One?
   A: Safety car **B:** Scoreboard correction **C:** Sharp corner

3. What does 'GP' stand for?
   A: Gravel pit **B:** Grip problem **C:** Grand Prix

4. What is the name for the position in front of all the other cars at the start of a race?
   A: Pole **B:** Leader **C:** Prime

5. What is the name for the area where cars can stop for refuelling, change tyres and make mechanical repairs?
   A: The Garage **B:** The Pits **C:** The Trailer Park

6. Which colour are the Ferrari F1 team associated with?
   A: Silver **B:** Blue **C:** Red

7. Pirelli are associated with which crucial part of an F1 car?
   A: Engine **B:** Tyres **C:** Bodywork

8. Drivers Michael Schumacher and Sebastian Vettel have represented which country?
   A: Germany **B:** Austria **C:** France

9. Ayrton Senna represented which country?
   A: Argentina **B:** Brazil **C:** Chile

10. In which decade was the inaugural season of F1?
A: 1890s **B:** 1950s **C:** 1990s

11. What is the name for a tight sequence of corners in alternate directions?
A: Twist **B:** Chicane **C:** Snake

12. What is the name of the three high-ranking officials appointed to make decisions at F1 races?
A: Stewards **B:** Umpires **C:** Referees

13. In which of the following countries has never held a Formula One race?
A: New Zealand **B:** Italy **C:** England

14. Jackie Stewart and Jim Clark are both F1 legends from which country?
A: Ireland **B:** Scotland **C:** USA

15. In which country is the famous race track Monza located?
A: Brazil **B:** Italy **C:** France

16. What is the correct surname of this former F1 world champion, Jenson …?
A: Button **B:** Butter **C:** Bottom

17. In which year did Lewis Hamilton win his first Formula One race?
A: 1997 **B:** 2007 **C:** 2017

18. Who is the only driver other than Lewis Hamilton to win the World Championship between 2014 and 2020?
A: Jacques Villeneuve **B:** Nigel Mansell **C:** Nico Rosberg

19. Which of the following constructors have never produced a Formula One winning car?
A: Toyota **B:** Honda **C:** Renault

20. What was the name of the legendary F1 commentator, who began his career with the BBC in the late 1940s and retired from full-time commentary in 2001?
A: Johnny Walker **B:** Murray Walker **C:** Brett Walker

21. Which Formula One team is based in the town of Maranello?
A: Mercedes **B:** Ferrari **C:** McLaren

22. Which British business magnate served as chief executive of the Formula One Group until 2017?
A: Alan Sugar **B:** Peter Jones **C:** Bernie Ecclestone

23. Which of the following is a famous F1 track?
A: Cheltenham **B:** Silverstone **C:** Goodwood

24. To signal the commencement of an F1 race, how many red starting lights go out?
A: 5 **B:** 10 **C:** 15

25. Which number is the reigning champion permitted to use (although not all choose to do so) on their car for the following season?
A: 0 **B:** 1 **C:** 2

F1 (MEDIUM)

BLACK FLAGS

This is the flag that spells doom for an F1 driver – it means you've been disqualified from the race and it has only ever been displayed a handful of times. Can you name the drivers responsible for these infamous moments?

1. Who was black flagged during the 2004 US Grand Prix for infringing the rules regarding his spare car and also at the 2005 Canadian Grand Prix for exiting the pits while the red light was flashing?
2. Who was black flagged in 1988 at his home Grand Prix after a mechanical failure in his first car meant that he had to change to the spare after the end of the formation lap?
3. Who was black flagged at the 1994 British Grand Prix for overtaking Damon Hill during the formation lap and failing to serve the stop-go penalty?
4. Who started his race from the pits in his spare car at the 1986 Italian Grand Prix five seconds after the green flag had been shown to start the formation lap?
5. Who was shown a black flag after he overshot his pit crew's position and reversed his car into place at the Portuguese GP in 1989?

1980s

1. Who became the first driver to win the World Championship with the Williams team, a feat he achieved in 1980?
2. Which circuit held the British Grand Prix in 1980, 1982, 1984 and 1986?
3. Which Brazilian driver won his first drivers' championship in 1981, beating Carlos Reutemann by a single point?
4. Which two drivers were separated by half a point in the final standings of the 1984 F1 drivers' World Championship?
5. Which driver's first win came at the torrentially wet 1985 Portuguese GP at Estoril, a race he won by over a minute?
6. Which driver earned his maiden victory in his 72nd start in F1 at the European GP in 1985?
7. It's 1988 and the drivers' championship goes down to the wire between two fierce competitors. Who were they?
8. Which Austrian driver became teammates at Ferrari for the 1989 F1 season with Nigel Mansell?

POINTS

How many points are currently awarded to drivers finishing in the first three places?

1. 1st: ________
2. 2nd: ________
3. 3rd: ________

NAME THOSE CHAMPIONS

1. Who won five World Championships in the 1950s and holds the record of winning the highest percentage of F1 races he entered?
2. Who finally won the drivers' championship in 1992 having finished as runner-up in 1986, 1987 and 1991?

3. Whose two titles were won back-to-back in 2005 and 2006?
4. Which legend won his three championships in 1988, 1990 and 1991?
5. Which two father-and-son pairings have won the Formula One drivers' championship?
6. Which former champion's father finished second in the 1979 drivers' championship?
7. Which Brit won the 2009 drivers' championship with a brand new team?
8. Which British driver won the World Championship in 1976, retired in 1979 and worked as a racing commentator for the BBC until his death in 1993?
9. Which four-time world champion won his first title in 1985?
10. Which two drivers and former world champions both won a record 13 races in a single season?

TRIVIA

1. Which British former F1 world champion only passed his driving test aged 24 and entered motorsport the following year?
2. Which three races together constitute the Triple Crown of Motorsport?
3. Which Brit finished as championship runner-up four times and in third place three times during a seven-year period between 1955 and 1961?
4. Which British driver finished runner-up in the 1999 F1 World Championship behind Mika Häkkinen?
5. At just 3.340 km long, which track is the shortest in the current F1 calendar?
6. Which F1 driver, who began his F1 career for Sauber in 2018, was born in Monaco?
7. Who became the youngest ever driver to start an F1 race, which he did aged 17 years and 166 days at the Australian GP in 2015?

8. How many cars started the 2005 US Grand Prix after seven teams refused to participate after stating concern about the quality of their Michelin tyres?
9. Who switched from F1 to IndyCar in 1993 and won the Championship?
10. Which type of tyre was banned from use in F1 from 1998 to 2008?
11. Who said this: 'Racing, competing, is in my blood. It's part of me, it's part of my life; I've been doing it all my life. And it stands up before anything else.'

F1 (HARD)

HOST COUNTRIES

By the end of the 2021 Formula One season, 34 countries will have hosted a Formula One Grand Prix. Can you get them all from the first letters of the countries' names and the number of letters?

1. A _ _ _ _ _ _ _ _
2. A _ _ _ _ _ _ _ _
3. A _ _ _ _ _ _
4. A _ _ _ _ _ _ _ _ _
5. B _ _ _ _ _ _
6. B _ _ _ _ _ _
7. B _ _ _ _ _
8. C _ _ _ _ _
9. C _ _ _ _
10. F _ _ _ _ _
11. G _ _ _ _ _ _
12. H _ _ _ _ _ _
13. I _ _ _ _
14. I _ _ _ _
15. J _ _ _ _
16. M _ _ _ _ _ _ _
17. M _ _ _ _ _
18. M _ _ _ _ _
19. M _ _ _ _ _ _
20. N _ _ _ _ _ _ _ _ _ _
21. P _ _ _ _ _ _ _
22. R _ _ _ _ _
23. S _ _   _ _ _ _ _ _
24. S _ _ _ _   _ _ _ _ _ _
25. S _ _ _ _ _ _ _ _
26. S _ _ _ _   _ _ _ _ _ _
27. S _ _ _ _   _ _ _ _ _
28. S _ _ _ _
29. S _ _ _ _ _
30. S _ _ _ _ _ _ _ _ _ _
31. T _ _ _ _ _
32. U _ _ _ _ _   _ _ _ _   _ _ _ _ _ _ _ _
33. U _ _ _ _ _   _ _ _ _ _ _ _
34. U _ _ _ _ _   _ _ _ _ _ _

TEAMMATES

1. Can you name Lewis Hamilton's five teammates from his debut in 2007 to today?
2. Can you recall Sebastian Vettel's five teammates from 2009 to today?

TRIVIA

1. Which German driver, active between 2000 and 2011, achieved the most podium finishes (13) without ever winning a race?
2. When was the last season in which an F1 car bore the starting number 1?
3. Who finished in second place at the BBC Sports Personality of the Year (SPOTY) Awards in 1957?
4. Who won SPOTY in 1994 and 1996?
5. Can you name the four F1 drivers who have been knighted?
6. Four circuits have held over 50 Grand Prix. Can you get them all?
7. In which year was Brands Hatch last used for the British Grand Prix?
8. Who won the final British Grand Prix at Brands Hatch?
9. In which English county will you find Silverstone?
10. Which current driver bears the number 44 on his car?
11. Nigel Mansell raced with which distinctive red number on the front of his car?
12. Ahead of the 2021 season, Champagne was replaced with which drink for the traditional podium celebrations?
13. Which two drivers have reached the podium 68 and 62 times respectively, but never won a World Championship?
14. Which driver ended up in Monaco harbour in 1955 in his Lancia D50?
15. Which driver recorded his only win at the 1971 Italian GP, in which he triumphed by 0.01 seconds, the closest finish in an F1 race?

16. Which driver beat British legend Jackie Stewart to the 1974 drivers' championship despite Stewart winning the last two races of the season?
17. Who famously pushed his car over the line at the 1959 US GP after his Cooper T51 ran out of fuel on the last lap?
18. Who made his Formula One debut for Jordan-Ford at the 1991 Belgian GP replacing the imprisoned French driver Bertrand Gachot?
19. As of 2001, F1 engines are limited to a maximum of how many rpm?
20. Which English racing driver won the 24 Hours of Le Mans in 1991 and finished fourth in the 1995 F1 drivers' championship?
21. Which constructor was victorious in the inaugural 1950 Formula One season?
22. Whose first F1 race win, recorded at the German GP in 2000, was made all the more memorable by the fact that the driver began the race in 18th place?
23. Who earned his first podium finish at the French GP in 1992 (eight years after his first start in F1), which was won by compatriot Nigel Mansell?
24. Which four teams did Juan Manuel Fangio win his five championships with?
25. Who had to wait until his 190th race – the 2020 Sakhir GP – to win his first F1 race?

GOLF

(ANSWERS PAGE 267)

See if your knowledge comes to the fore or whether you find yourself swinging and missing in this section that ranges from an easy pitch and putt to an approach shot at the Road Hole in a Force 9 gale while playing with a hickory shafted four iron. talk-SPORT covers the best of the action at all the majors, so see how you get on with these.

GOLF (EASY)

TRIVIA

1. How many holes are there in a standard round of golf?
   A: 12 **B:** 18 **C:** 24

2. The three basic types of golf clubs are:
   A: Woods, irons and a putter **B:** Leads, steels and a putter
   C: Whackers, whooshers and a putter

3. What is a golf club designed to extricate a golfer from a bunker known as?
   A: Sand wedge **B:** Sand shovel **C:** Mashie niblick

4. What is the name of the person who carries a professional golf player's clubs and offers advice?
   A: Footman **B:** Caddie **C:** Valet

5. What is the warning call that a player will shout if he or she has accidentally hit a ball towards players or spectators?
   A: Incoming! **B:** Ahoy! **C:** Fore!

6. What is the name for a golf course located close to the coast, typically on sand dunes?
   A: Links **B:** Pinks **C:** Winks

7. What is the name of the specially kept area around a golf hole where a player putts?
   A: Park **B:** Common **C:** Green

8. In which country is the oldest golf course in the world?
   A: USA **B:** Scotland **C:** Ireland

9. What does O.B. stand for?
   A: Odd Bounce **B:** Older Ball **C:** Out of Bounds

10. The number of strokes that a golfer should need to complete a hole is known by what three-letter name?
    A: Cut **B:** Par **C:** Tap

11. What is the missing word: Birdie, _________, Albatross?
    A: Hawk **B:** Falcon **C:** Eagle

12. The player who achieved the best score on the previous hole is allowed to play first on the next hole. But what is this ritual known as?
    A: The honour **B:** The privilege **C:** The entitlement

13. The small wooden or plastic stand used to strike a golf ball is known by what name?
    A: Splint **B:** Tee **C:** Holder

14. A facility in which golfers are able to practise hitting the ball is known as a what?
    A: Shooting range **B:** Driving range **C:** Striking range

15. By the time of his election as US president, who owned 17 golf courses?
    A: Bill Clinton **B:** George W. Bush **C:** Donald Trump

16. A piece of turf removed from the ground by a golf club striking it is known by which name?
    A: Tuft **B:** Divot **C:** Lump

17. Which US president famously said 'Now watch this drive' from a golf course after making a statement about suicide bombers in the Middle East in 2002?
    A: Bill Clinton **B:** Jimmy Carter **C:** George W. Bush

18. Which film involves Adam Sandler playing a failed ice hockey player who realises he has a talent for golf?
    A: *Happy Gilmore* **B:** *Tin Cup* **C:** *The Legend of Bagger Vance*

19. In which film does Bill Murray frantically try to hunt down a gopher that is tearing up a golf course?
A: *Field of Dreams* **B:** *Caddyshack* **C:** *The Rookie*

20. The champion of the annual Masters Tournament in the USA receives which distinctive item of clothing?
A: Red hat **B:** Yellow gloves **C:** Green jacket

GOLF (MEDIUM)

NICKNAMES

Can you match the famous nicknames with the golfers?

1. El Niño	Ian Poulter
2. Golden Bear	Ernie Els
3. Great White Shark	Fred Couples
4. Lefty	Greg Norman
5. Walrus	Jack Nicklaus
6. Wild Thing	Arnold Palmer
7. The Big Easy	Sergio García
8. Boom Boom	Phil Mickelson
9. The King	John Daly
10. The Postman	Craig Stadler

NATIONAL FIRSTS

Can you name the first players from each of the countries below to win a major?

1. Germany ________________
2. Wales ________________
3. Canada ________________
4. Fiji ________________
5. Rep. of Ireland ________________
6. Sweden ________________
7. Italy ________________
8. Japan ________________

RYDER CUP CAPTAINS

Can you remember the previous ten Ryder Cup captains from their initials?

Year	Europe	US
2020 (21)	P. H.	S. S.
2018	T. B.	J. F.
2016	D. C.	D. L.
2014	P. M.	T. W.
2012	J. M. O.	D. L.
2010	C. M.	C. P.
2008	N. F.	P. A.
2006	I. W.	T. L.
2004	B. L.	H. S.
2002	S. T.	C. S.
1999	M. J.	B. C.

MOST WEEKS AT NUMBER ONE

Can you work out the five golfers who have spent the most weeks holding the number one ranking from the clues below?

Weeks at No. 1	Clue	Name
683	Winner of 15 majors, the last of which (as at July 2021) was the 2019 Masters	
331	Australian legend who won The Open in 1986 and 1993	
127	American who won the US Open in 2016 and the Masters in 2020	
106	Northern Irishman who won his first major in 2011	
97	Englishman who won the Masters back to back in 1989 and 1990	

THE MAJORS

1. Can you arrange the four major golf championships in calendar order?
2. Can you arrange the four major golf championships in order of the years in which they were founded, from oldest to most recent?

GOLF (HARD)

ONLY THREE ...

1. Only three players had won four major tournaments by the time they turned 25. Who are they?
2. Only three golfers have reached number one in the world rankings either without ever winning a major or before winning their first major. Who are they?

OPEN VENUES

Can you name the ten courses that are selected from as venues for The Open?

1.	______________________	6.	______________________
2.	______________________	7.	______________________
3.	______________________	8.	______________________
4.	______________________	9.	______________________
5.	______________________	10.	______________________

ANAGRAMS

Can you unscramble the anagrams to reveal the names of ten famous golfers?

1. KIMCHI POLLENS
2. GOOD WRITES
3. CAIRO SAGGIER
4. DIJON NOSHNUTS
5. COYLY MIRROR
6. TOWELED WOES
7. HARPED JOINTS
8. ABBA BOWNUTS
9. JOINT USERS
10. MINTY EARMARK

Can you identify the legendary golf courses hiding among the jumbled letters?

1. ANATOLIAN AUGUST
2. BABBLE CHEEP
3. SAGS WARS
4. EMIR FLUID
5. BURR ENTRY
6. RECUSATION
7. ORTON
8. HEN MAID
9. ARMED LARVA
10. STRAINS TWILIGHTS

GOLF AROUND THE WORLD

According to the R&A's 'Golf Around the World' report in 2019, 78% of the golf courses in the world are located in just ten countries. Can you name all the countries?

1. ______________________
2. ______________________
3. ______________________
4. ______________________
5. ______________________
6. ______________________
7. ______________________
8. ______________________
9. ______________________
10. ______________________

CAREER GRAND SLAM

American golfer of the 1920s and 1930s Gene Sarazen was the first player to win all four of the majors in his career. Four other players have achieved this feat (as at the start of 2022). Can you name them?

1. ______________________
2. ______________________
3. ______________________
4. ______________________

TRIVIA

1. In which year was the first Ryder Cup to include players from Continental Europe?
2. Who was the youngest ever Ryder Cup captain when he was appointed for the 1963 event?

3. What little bit of golf history unites Princess Anne, Laura Davies and Annika Sörenstam?
4. Which is the only golf club in the British Isles granted permission during the reign of Elizabeth II to include the appellation 'Royal'?
5. The Walker Cup is contested in odd-numbered years by amateur players belonging to which two teams?
6. Who won gold at the 2016 Olympics in the men's individual golf event?
7. Which golfer finished second at the BBC Sports Personality of the Year Awards in 2006 and 2011?
8. Which golfer won SPOTY in 1989?
9. 'Amen Corner' refers to which three holes at Augusta National?
10. Which golfer has played the most Ryder Cups?
11. Who became the youngest golfer to play a Ryder Cup, aged 19 years and 258 days in 1999?
12. Who famously holed a 65-ft putt to force a play-off at the 1995 Open Championship at St Andrews?
13. Who holed the putt to retain the 2012 Ryder Cup and complete the 'Miracle at Medinah'?
14. Who holed a 10-ft putt at the 18th at Augusta to become the first Briton to win the Masters in 1988?
15. By how many shots did Tiger Woods win the 2000 US Open?

WOMEN'S GOLF

1. What are the five women's major golf championships?
2. Who won a record 15 major titles and became the LPGA's first president?
3. Who retired from professional golf in 2008 with a record of 90 international tournament wins to her name including ten majors?

4. Who was given a sponsor's exemption to play in the 2004 Sony Open, becoming the youngest woman to play a PGA tour event, aged just 14?
5. Who is the only golfer to receive a damehood for services to golf?
6. Who won the gold in the Golf individual event at the 2016 Olympics, the first women's golf event since 1900?

HORSE RACING

(ANSWERS PAGE 273)

Not content with covering the Grand National, Royal Ascot, Cheltenham and the Derby, we picked up the pace here at talkSPORT, becoming a principal partner of 2021's inaugural Racing League with a team of jockeys managed by broadcasting legends Alan Brazil and Rupert Bell. So, do you fancy yourself as a front runner, a steady and stable rider or a dark horse for this section?

HORSE RACING (EASY)

TRIVIA

1. Which of the following is a unit of distance commonly used in horse racing?
   A: Metre **B:** Furlong **C:** League
2. Which of the following is an expression used to describe the surface of a horse-racing track before a race?
   A: Offing **B:** Running **C:** Going
3. What is the name of the headgear worn by horses to limit their vision and reduce distractions?
   A: Peepers **B:** Hoods **C:** Blinkers
4. What is the name for the enclosure where horses are saddled and paraded before a race?
   A: Paddock **B:** Quarters **C:** Box
5. Which month does the Grand National take place in?
   A: January **B:** April **C:** September
6. At which racecourse is the Grand National held?
   A: Brighton **B:** Musselburgh **C:** Aintree
7. At which racecourse would you find the royal enclosure?
   A: Ascot **B:** Wolverhampton **C:** Great Yarmouth
8. According to the Ascot official website, approximately how many Champagne bottles are consumed each year over the course of the five-day race meeting?
   A: 560 **B:** 5,600 **C:** 56,000

9. What is the name for a female horse aged four years and younger?
   A: Filly **B:** Gilly **C:** Tilly

10. In which country does the Kentucky Derby take place?
    A: USA **B:** Ireland **C:** Argentina

11. Which of the following is the name of a legendary racehorse?
    A: Violet Vodka **B:** Green Gin **C:** Red Rum

12. Which of the following was a champion racehorse in the 1930s and the subject of a 1999 film?
    A: Seabiscuit **B:** Reservoir cracker **C:** Rivercookie

13. Spot the real jockey hidden among the fake names.
    A: Frankie Delabour **B:** Frankie Dettori
    C: Frankie Degreen

14. The Epsom Downs Racecourse is famously associated with which race?
    A: The Dartford **B:** The Derby **C:** The Dover

HORSE RACING (MEDIUM)

GRAND NATIONAL

1. Who made history in 2021 by becoming the first female jockey to win the Grand National?
2. Which was the only year in which the Grand National was declared void after 30 of the 39 riders did not see the recall flag?
3. What is the name of the fence that is jumped as the 6th and 22nd fence in the race?
4. What is the name of the 15th fence, the tallest on the course?
5. Which is the only horse to have been ridden to victory on three occasions?
6. Which UK city is closest to the racecourse?
7. Who became the first woman to train a Grand National winner when Corbiere won in 1983?

ANAGRAMS

Can you unscramble the letters to reveal the names of these famous racecourses?

1. COAST
2. REXTEE
3. RUBY WEN
4. ETCHERS
5. RETINAE
6. ANTHEM LECH
7. NOTED CARS
8. KNEW TAMER
9. ELECT SWAN
10. DODO GO OW
11. OUTER TEXT
12. ALFRED KIPLING
13. DEMON SWOPS
14. CHOP DARK YAK
15. KART MONK PEP
16. ONWARD SPANK

TRIVIA

1. Jockeys wearing racing colours comprising a purple jacket with gold braid, scarlet sleeves and a gold-fringed black velvet cap are owned by whom?
2. Which commentator, dubbed the 'Voice of Racing', was knighted in 1997, the year he retired?
3. Who became the first jockey to win BBC Sports Personality of the Year, a feat he achieved in 2010?
4. Which horse-racing pundit and *Celebrity Big Brother* contestant died in 2019?
5. Which television channel took over broadcasting rights of the Grand National in 2013?
6. Which commercial radio station became the first to broadcast the Grand National in 2014?
7. The King George VI and Queen Elizabeth Stakes are run at which racecourse?
8. Which racecourse does the Champion Hurdle take place at?

FAMOUS OWNERS

1. Which former football manager part-owned the horse Rock of Gibraltar, the 2002 European horse of the year?
2. The Queen bought the filly Memory for £500,000 in 2011, which was part-owned by which British actress?
3. Which legendary rock guitarist owns the horse Sandymount Duke, which won its first race in 2014?
4. Who bought a racehorse in 2012 for £63,000, which he named Switcharooney?
5. Which former England footballer owned the racehorse Brown Panther which won the Goodwood Cup in 2013 and the Irish St Leger in 2014?

HORSE RACING (HARD)

ANAGRAMS

Can you find the names of the famous jockeys hidden among the jungled letters?

1. TIPSTER TOGGLE
2. KART RENOTIFIED
3. CAM COPY
4. OLEFIN RANKLE
5. BRUSHY LAW
6. CHEF JAN MORON
7. LOCALISER WIN
8. DATED PREY
9. CORRODING SHARD
10. ACUTE SEVENTH

GRAND NATIONAL

1. What links the following five Grand National winners: Tipperary Tim, Gregalach, Caughoo, Foinavon and Mon Mome?
2. What is the fewest number of horses to finish a Grand National?
3. What was the name of the horse that was leading the 1956 Grand National but jumped in the air and landed on its stomach just 40 yards from the finishing line?
4. Which jockey has ridden the Grand National 21 times between 1997 and 2019 without winning?
5. In the two years that Red Rum entered the race but didn't win the Grand National, which position did he finish in both times?

NAME THAT HORSE

Can you work out which famous horses the clues are referring to? (The clues are in two or more parts, which relate to a syllable or part of the answer.)

1. French for 'expensive' | one of the first sounds a baby makes
2. Noise emitted by an old-fashioned steam train | type of coat
3. Abandon someone in a difficult situation | fantastical evil creature that serves Sauron | sought cover
4. Highest quality | merchant vessel officer
5. Subtract | passenger compartment of a railway carriage | collect £200 for passing here
6. Famous cartoon character who wears a red bow | patriarch and Springfield resident
7. Green and yellow wire | total amount | glove used in baseball
8. Element AU | mammal's home | a person who crushes grain into flour

TRIVIA

1. Which racecourse acted as a replacement host in 2005 for Royal Ascot while Ascot racecourse was closed for redevelopment?
2. The first race meeting was held at Ascot in 1711 during the reign of which monarch?
3. At which of the Queen's residences is the Royal Studs located?
4. Which is the only horse to have won four consecutive Ascot Gold Cups?
5. Which is the longest professional flat race in Britain, which takes place at Ascot in June?
6. Which horse won the Derby in 1981 by a record 10 lengths?
7. Can you name the only two jockeys who have ever been knighted?

8. Which horse won the Cheltenham Gold Cup for three consecutive years between 2002 and 2004?
9. Which company serves as the main auctioneer of the race horses in the UK and Ireland?
10. Which former leading amateur flat jockey and Champion Lady Rider made her debut as a television presenter in 1995, introducing highlights of Royal Ascot?
11. Which five races constitute the 'British Classics'?
12. Which three races comprise the Triple Crown of Thoroughbred Racing in the USA?

RUGBY LEAGUE

(ANSWERS PAGE 278)

We're an official radio broadcaster of all things Super League. talkSPORT's Mark Wilson gives the punters what they want with live match action and an even livelier phone-in. So whether you fancy a gentle kick over the posts or a scrum down with Sinfield, we've got a little something for everyone in this section.

RUGBY LEAGUE (EASY)

TRIVIA

1. How many players make up a rugby league side?
   A: 8 **B:** 13 **C:** 18

2. How many of these players comprise the forwards?
   A: 2 **B:** 4 **C:** 6

3. How many points is a try worth?
   A: 4 **B:** 10 **C:** 15

4. How many points is a penalty worth?
   A: 1 **B:** 2 **C:** 5

5. Spot the incorrectly named club team in the selection of three below?
   A: Warrington Wolves **B:** Castleford Caterpillars
   C: Leeds Rhinos

6. What is the name of the main knockout tournament organised by the Rugby Football League?
   A: The Determination Cup **B:** The Fortitude Cup
   C: The Challenge Cup

7. An attacking team is allowed a maximum of how many tackles to progress up the field of play?
   A: Six **B:** Sixteen **C:** Twenty-six

8. What is the top tier of rugby league in Britain called?
   A: Big League **B:** Premier League **C:** Super League

9. Which English county was the first rugby league match played in?
   A: Yorkshire **B:** Suffolk **C:** Cornwall

10. How many minutes are there in each half of a rugby league game?
    A: 20 **B:** 40 **C:** 60

11. In which year was the first Rugby League World Cup held?
    A: 1754 **B:** 1854 **C:** 1954

12. Which of the following is the correctly named rugby league star?
    A: Kevin Saintfield **B:** Kevin Sinfield **C:** Kevin Wrongfield

13. When was the women's Rugby League World Cup instituted?
    A: 1900 **B:** 1950 **C:** 2000

14. The Rugby League World Cup was stolen from the Midland Hotel in Bradford in 1970 and was not seen again for 20 years.
    A: True **B:** False

INTERNATIONAL TEAM NICKNAMES

Match the nickname to the international team:

1. Kangaroos	England
2. Lions	United States
3. Wolfhounds	Russia
4. Cedars	Australia
5. Bears	Canada
6. Tomahawks	Ireland
7. Wolverines	Lebanon

RUGBY LEAGUE (MEDIUM)

CLUB MIX-UP

The names of these Super League clubs have got mixed up. Can you put the second part of their names with the correct first parts?

1. Castleford Rhinos
2. Catalans Centurions
3. Huddersfield Red Devils
4. Hull Kingston Warriors
5. Leeds Tigers
6. Leigh Wolves
7. Salford Giants
8. Wigan Dragons
9. Wakefield Rovers
10. Warrington Trinity

CODE SWAPPERS

Can you identify these players who switched from League to Union or vice versa?

1. This League and Union legend, and one of only 21 players to win multiple Rugby Union World Cups, became New Zealand's Heavyweight Boxing Champion in 2012.
2. This full-back and winger made his senior League career with Wigan Warriors, shifted to Union in 2007 and finished the 2011 World Cup as joint top try-scorer.
3. A centre/wing who was born a New Zealander but gained dual nationality in 2010 and was called up by Martin Johnson to join England's squad that same year. He started all five games in the 2011 Six Nations.
4. Became the youngest ever captain of the Great Britain Rugby League side aged 21, in 1996; retired from League in 2005 to join Saracens and made his international Union debut in 2007 in the Six Nations against Scotland.

5. Nicknamed the 'Volcano', this winger has played sevens for Tonga, League for New Zealand and Union for England, on top of scoring 149 tries in 152 appearances for the Bradford Bulls before moving to Gloucester in 2007.
6. This second-row played League from 1994 to 2000 for the Brisbane Broncos and broke into the Australia side in 1998 before switching to Union in 2001 and going on to play for the All Blacks, starting the 2011 World Cup Final.
7. Wigan legend from 1991 to 2000, this flying full-back went on to become England's first black rugby union captain in 2004.
8. Scorer of over 500 tries in his League career, which England and Great Britain winger joined Widnes for a world record fee of £440,000, before finally finishing his career with rugby union side Wasps?

TRIVIA

1. Who is the host country for the men's, women's and wheelchair Rugby League World Cups that were postponed from 2021 to 2022?
2. Name the three teams that have won the Rugby League World Cup.
3. Which club won eight Challenge Cups in a row between 1987 and 1995?
4. Rugby League has been traditionally associated with towns along the corridor of which motorway?
5. Headingley is a stadium associated with which rugby league club?

RUGBY LEAGUE (HARD)

Can you name the 14 teams that competed in the 2017 Rugby League World Cup?

1. ____________________ 8. ____________________
2. ____________________ 9. ____________________
3. ____________________ 10. ____________________
4. ____________________ 11. ____________________
5. ____________________ 12. ____________________
6. ____________________ 13. ____________________
7. ____________________ 14. ____________________

CHALLENGE CUP SPONSORSHIP

Amazingly, the first two sponsors of the Challenge Cup were cigarette brands State Express and Silk Cut. Can you name the six sponsors of the Challenge Cup from 2002 to 2020?

1. 2002–2003 ____________ 4. 2013–2014 ____________
2. 2004–2007 ____________ 5. 2015–2018 ____________
3. 2008–2012 ____________ 6. 2019–2020 ____________

TRIVIA

1. Which club team became the first from North America to compete in the Super League?
2. In which town was the Northern Rugby Football Union formed, considered to be the birth of rugby league?
3. In which year was the last Challenge Cup played at the old Wembley stadium, before it closed for redevelopment?

4. Since the millennium, three English players have won the Golden Boot. Can you name them?
5. The World Cup draw for the 2021 event took place at Buckingham Palace in January 2020, but which member of the royal family, the Rugby Football League's patron, hosted it?
6. Who are the only professional rugby league team in the south of England?
7. Which French rugby league team, one of the founding members of the Super League, was dissolved in 1997?
8. Which stadium has hosted the Super League Grand Final every year since 1998 except for in 2020?
9. Which stadium hosted the 2020 Super League Grand Final?
10. The Lance Todd trophy is awarded to whom?
11. Who succeeded ex-footballer Tony Adams as President of the Rugby Football League in 2020?
12. Which team lost five consecutive Super League Grand Finals between 2007 and 2011?
13. Which Australian club won the World Club Challenge in 2019 and 2020?

SUPER LEAGUE TOP SCORERS

Can you fill in the list of top scorers in the Super League from the clues provided?

Player	Points	Club(s)	Career Span
	3,443	Leeds	1997–2015
	2,462	Hull FC, Huddersfield, Wakefield	2005–2006, 2008–2020
	2,415	Oldham, Bradford, Wigan	1997–2011
	2,372	Wigan	1996–2004
	2,280	Wigan, Catalans	2006–2013, 2016

RUGBY UNION

(ANSWERS PAGE 282)

As the exclusive radio broadcaster, we've roared on the Lions over the years and 2021 was no exception. Our brilliant commentary team led by Andrew McKenna, World Cup winner Ben Kay and Lions legend Sir Ian McGeechan would know the answers to these questions. So, put your scrum cap on, get your head down and grab the shorts in front of you. Use it or lose it!

RUGBY UNION (EASY)

TERMS AND RULES

1. How many points does a team score for a try?
   A: Five **B:** Ten **C:** Fifteen

2. How many points are scored from a penalty?
   A: One **B:** Three **C:** Ten

3. What is the name for the kick that takes place after a try is scored?
   A: Side Kick **B:** Conversion **C:** Free Kick

4. How many players make up a rugby union team?
   A: 15 **B:** 19 **C:** 22

5. What is the name of the yearly competition between the teams of England, Wales, Scotland, France, Ireland and Italy?
   A: Six Nations Championship **B:** European Championship **C:** Cross Channel Championships

6. What rough shape is a rugby union ball?
   A: Circular **B:** Oval **C:** Triangular

7. What is the name for the variant of rugby union that was contested in the Summer Olympics for the first time in 2016?
   A: Rugby Fives **B:** At Sixes and Sevens **C:** Rugby Sevens

8. What is the name for the interlocked formation of players that attempt to gain possession of the ball after restarting play?
   A: Fracas **B:** Rabble **C:** Scrum

9. What is the correct name for the rugby position?
   A: Fly-Half **B:** Bee Half **C:** Wasp Half

10. Which letter do the posts at each end of a rugby pitch resemble?
    A: I **B:** H **C:** T

11. Which is the real rugby position lurking among the fake ones?
    A: Hooker **B:** Midfield Defence **C:** Line Backer

12. How long does a rugby union match last?
    A: 60 minutes **B:** 80 minutes **C:** 99 minutes

13. What is the name for the area outside the two lines that run lengthways along a rugby pitch?
    A: Touch **B:** Taste **C:** Smell

14. When a player is cautioned with a yellow card, they are sent to which area?
    A: Infraction Station **B:** Sin Bin **C:** Punishment Dump

NICKNAMES

Match the nicknames for these men's rugby teams with the teams:

1. New Zealand	Brave Blossoms
2. Australia	Los Pumas
3. Japan	All Blacks
4. Argentina	Springboks
5. South Africa	Wallabies

SHIRTS

Match the home colour of the jerseys the team wears with the team:

1. England	Black
2. Scotland	Red
3. Australia	Red and white hoops
4. Japan	Green
5. New Zealand	Light blue and white hoops
6. Argentina	Yellow
7. Wales	White
8. Ireland	Dark blue

STADIUMS

Match the stadiums to the teams that commonly play their home games there:

1. Murrayfield	Wales
2. Twickenham	South Africa
3. Millennium Stadium	Ireland
4. Lansdowne Road (Aviva Stadium)	Italy
5. Stadio Olimpico	England
6. Ellis Park	Scotland

TRUE OR FALSE

1. You are permitted to pass the ball forwards and backwards in rugby.
2. England have never won the Rugby World Cup.
3. The first rules for rugby were written at Rugby School in Warwickshire.
4. The first Rugby World Cup was held in 2003.
5. Saracens and Harlequins are the names of England rugby union club teams.

6. The England rugby union team's emblem is a red rose.
7. The Welsh rugby union team's emblem is a leek.

TRIVIA

1. What is the name for the traditional Māori dance that takes place before New Zealand play an international match?
   A: Hangi **B:** Hapu **C:** Haka

2. The first rugby union international match took place between England and which country?
   A: China **B:** Scotland **C:** Panama

3. Dan Carter is a famous player who played for which international team?
   A: South Africa **B:** New Zealand **C:** England

4. How many years usually separate World Cups?
   A: Four years **B:** Eight years **C:** Twelve years

5. Who was the supposed inventor of rugby?
   A: Winston Webb Wallace **B:** William Webb Ellis
   C: Walter Webb Harris

6. Which South African president attempted to use rugby to connect the people of South Africa after apartheid?
   A: Nelson Mandela **B:** Thabo Mbeki **C:** Jacob Zuma

7. Ex-England rugby player Mike Tindall married which member of the royal family?
   A: Zara Phillips **B:** Princess Eugenie of York
   C: Princess Beatrice of York

8. The touring side selected from the England, Scotland, Wales and Ireland rugby teams are referred to by what name?
   A: The Wolves **B:** The Lions **C:** The Roses

9. Who was voted BBC Sports Personality of the Year in 2003?
   A: Will Carling **B:** Bill Beaumont **C:** Jonny Wilkinson

10. Which former England captain was one of the team captains on *A Question of Sport* from 1982 to 1996?
A: Bill Beaumont **B:** Rob Andrew **C:** Phil de Glanville

RUGBY UNION (MEDIUM)

MOST CAPPED ENGLAND PLAYERS

Can you work out the names of the most capped England players of all time from the clues?

1. Prop from 1990 to 2004 and later RFU president.
2. Still-playing scrum-half with a brother who was also capped for England.
3. Hooker from 2008 to 2018 and former England captain.
4. Long-serving Leicester Tigers tighthead prop; first played for England in 2010.
5. Fly-half who scored his 1,000th Test point in February 2021.
6. World-cup winning fly-half.
7. Versatile 6ft 7in lock/flanker first capped for England in 2009.

SYLLABLE GAME

Work out the names of these rugby legends from the clues that make up the syllables of their names:

1. Impair | Silvery metal associated with Cornwall | US slang for toilet | Male offspring
2. Martial arts rank | Automobile | Northern slang for 'thanks'
3. Abundant | Vital energy | Waterproof raincoat | Sound a crow makes
4. Determination | Environmental | Area of growing trees
5. Glass container | US award for TV | Sudden rush of wind | Baby bed

6. Boyfriend | Somewhere thieves might congregate | A place you'd order a drink from | First name of Mr Butler in *Gone with the Wind*
7. Spend time ineffectually | Nickname for Richard | Admin worker in an office
8. Steal | Point on a compass | Hill or peak in south-west England
9. To cook slowly in liquid | Creative activity | Monopolise something unfairly
10. Tease someone playfully | Toilet | Perceive

TROPHIES

Can you match up the pairs of teams that contest each one of these trophies?

1. Calcutta Cup	Australia and South Africa
2. Auld Alliance Trophy	New Zealand and Australia
3. Giuseppe Garibaldi Trophy	Australia and Scotland
4. Centenary Quaich	Australia and Argentina
5. Doddie Weir Cup	Wales and South Africa
6. Bledisloe Cup	Ireland and Scotland
7. Mandela Challenge Plate	England and Scotland
8. Freedom Cup	Australia and England
9. Cook Cup	Scotland and Wales
10. Puma Trophy	Australia and France
11. Trophée des Bicentenaires	New Zealand and South Africa
12. Lansdowne Cup	New Zealand and England
13. Hopetoun Cup	Scotland and France
14. Hillary Shield	Australia and Ireland
15. Prince William Cup	Italy and France

ANAGRAMS

Can you work out the names of these jumbled-up Premiership clubs?

1. SWAPS
2. ROB SLIT
3. HERN QUAILS
4. NIL DISHONOR
5. CORSET GLUE
6. HEFTIER EXECS
7. PHANTOMS STRONTIAN
8. ELECT REGISTRIES
9. ACESCENT SNOWFALL
10. WRITER ACROSS ROWER

NUMBERS AND POSITIONS

Can you add the positions traditionally attached to the numbers below?

1. ______________________
2. ______________________
3. ______________________
4. ______________________
5. ______________________
6. ______________________
7. ______________________
8. ______________________
9. ______________________
10. ______________________
11. ______________________
12. ______________________
13. ______________________
14. ______________________
15. ______________________

TRIVIA

1. What does TMO stand for?
2. Which player was nicknamed the 'Raging Potato'?
3. Which referee, who holds the record for most Test matches refereed, retired in December 2020 after a 17-year career?
4. Which three Pacific nations traditionally compete in the Pacific Nations Cup?
5. The Rugby Championship is an annual competition between which four nations?
6. The 2019 Rugby World Cup was held in which country?

7. Which Welshman currently holds the record for most Test tries scored by an active player?
8. Who, in 2018, became the second Irishman to win World Rugby Player of the Year?
9. Who coached the British and Irish Lions on their tours to Australia in 2013 and New Zealand in 2017?
10. The Lions have worn which colour jersey since 1950?
11. England's victory over New Zealand in the 2019 World Cup semi-final was their first over the All Blacks since a resounding 38–21 win in which year?
12. How many drop-goal attempts did Jonny Wilkinson miss before he made his famous one in the last seconds of extra time in the 2003 World Cup Final?
13. Who is Will Carling describing here in 1995: 'I am hoping not to come across him again. He's a freak and the sooner he goes away the better.'
14. Which former rugby player became a permanent team captain of *A Question of Sport* in 2004?
15. Who presented Francois Pienaar with the Webb Ellis Cup in 1995?
16. Who played Francois Pienaar in the film *Invictus* in 2009?
17. Which former French rugby player was nicknamed l'Homme des Cavernes (the Caveman)?

RUGBY UNION (HARD)

LINE-UPS

Can you name the England XV that started the World Cup Final in 2019 against South Africa from their initials?

1. M.V.
2. J.G.
3. K.S.
4. M.I.
5. C.L.
6. T.C.
7. S.U.
8. B.V.
9. B.Y.
10. G.F.
11. J.M.
12. O.F.
13. M.T.
14. A.W.
15. E.D.

ANAGRAMS

Can you work out the names of these jumbled-up England rugby captains?

1. WONDERBRA
2. FALLEN ROWER
3. PRICKLY HIVE
4. CRAWLING ILL
5. ALBION TUMBLE
6. JINNAH MORTONS
7. JINNY KNOWS LION
8. ANALOGICAL DWELLER

HIGHEST POINTS SCORERS OF ALL TIME

Can you fill in the names of the highest international points scorers of all time from the clues in the table below? Note this includes points scored for the British Lions and the British & Irish Lions and is correct as at 1 September 2021.

Rank	Name	Points	Country	International Career Span
1		1,598	New Zealand	2003–15
2		1,246	England	1998–2011
3		1,090	Wales	1990–2003
4		1,083	Ireland	2000–2013
5		1,053	England	2012–
6		1,010	Italy and Argentina	1991–2003, 1989
7		970	Wales	1998–2011
8		967	New Zealand	1995–2004
9		930	Ireland	2009–
10		911	Australia	1984–1995

WORLD CUP 2019

Can you name all 20 teams that participated in the Rugby World Cup in 2019?

1. ____________________ 11. ____________________
2. ____________________ 12. ____________________
3. ____________________ 13. ____________________
4. ____________________ 14. ____________________
5. ____________________ 15. ____________________
6. ____________________ 16. ____________________
7. ____________________ 17. ____________________
8. ____________________ 18. ____________________
9. ____________________ 19. ____________________
10. ____________________ 20. ____________________

TOP-FLIGHT TEAMS

28 teams have played in rugby union's top flight in England. Can you name them all? We've given you the first letters and the number of seasons they've played in the top flight in brackets.

B (34)	L (8)	N (22)	R (2)
B (23)	L (34)	N (29)	S (28)
B (3)	L (2)	N (5)	S (29)
C (1)	L (26)	O (10)	W (34)
E (11)	L (2)	R (2)	W (2)
G (34)	L (2)	R (4)	W (5)
H (33)	M (4)	R (2)	W (15)

INDIVIDUAL AWARDS

1. Which hooker turned pundit was the inaugural winner of the World Rugby Men's 15s Player of the Year in 2001?
2. Which two All Blacks have won the World Rugby Men's 15s Player of the Year award three times each?
3. Which English rugby union coach was knighted in the 2004 New Year's Honours list?
4. Which former England rugby union captain received a knighthood in 2018 for services to the game?

EUROPEAN RUGBY CHAMPIONS CUP

Can you fill in the winning teams (known as the Heineken Cup between 1995 and 2014 and later the Heineken Champions Cup from 2018) from the scores and their opponents below for the last 10 finals?

1. 2011–2012 ________________ 42–14 Ulster
2. 2012–2013 ________________ 16–15 Clermont
3. 2013–2014 ________________ 23–6 Saracens
4. 2014–2015 ________________ 24–18 Clermont

5. 2015–2016 ______________ 21–9 Racing 92
6. 2016–2017 ______________ 28–17 Clermont
7. 2017–2018 ______________ 15–12 Racing 92
8. 2018–2019 ______________ 20–10 Leinster
9. 2019–2020 ______________ 31–27 Racing 92
10. 2020–2021 ______________ 22–17 La Rochelle

WORLD CUP FINALS

Can you fill in the teams who have contested each World Cup Final from the scores below?

1. 1987 ______________ 29–9 ______________
2. 1991 ______________ 12–6 ______________
3. 1995 ______________ 15–12 (aet) ______________
4. 1999 ______________ 35–12 ______________
5. 2003 ______________ 20–17 (aet) ______________
6. 2007 ______________ 15–6 ______________
7. 2011 ______________ 8–7 ______________
8. 2015 ______________ 34–17 ______________
9. 2019 ______________ 32–12 ______________

TRIVIA

1. Which two teams contested the Rugby Sevens final at the 2016 Olympics?
2. Which two teams contested the women's World Cup Final in 2017?
3. The inaugural women's World Cup saw England lose to which team 19–6?
4. The widest margin of victory in a World Cup game was 142 points, in 2003, but which two teams were involved?
5. The All Blacks put 145 points past which team at the 1995 World Cup?
6. Which three players have scored the most points at World Cups?

7. Which two legends of the game share the record for most tries scored at World Cups?
8. In which year did the Five Nations become the Six Nations?
9. Which four organisations have sponsored the Five/Six Nations tournament?
10. Which team achieved three Grand Slam wins in four years between 2017 and 2020 at the Women's Six Nations Championship?
11. Which invitational rugby club play in black and white hoops but with socks from players' own club strips?

TENNIS

(ANSWERS PAGE 291)

Whether you're a 'Wimbledon's on so I'll dust off my racket' sort of person or an 'all-weather warrior', we're hoping that you can ace these questions or, at the very least, avoid a straight sets drubbing. New balls please!

TENNIS (EASY)

TRIVIA

1. What is the name for a serve which lands in the service box and is not touched by the opponent?
   A: Queen **B:** King **C:** Ace

2. Who is the last British player to win Wimbledon?
   A: Andy Murray **B:** Tim Henman **C:** Greg Rusedski

3. What is the score 40–40 commonly known as?
   A: Break point **B:** Deuce **C:** Advantage

4. What does AELTC stand for?
   A: All England Lawn Tennis Club
   B: Amateur English Ladies Tennis Club
   C: Australian Exhibition Ladies Tennis Championships

5. What is the name for the official who enforces the rules of the game and typically sits in a high chair by the net?
   A: Referee **B:** Judge **C:** Umpire

6. Who famously screamed 'You cannot be serious!' at Wimbledon in 1981?
   A: John McEnroe **B:** Ivan Lendl **C:** Boris Becker

7. Roger Federer plays for which country?
   A: Germany **B:** Switzerland **C:** Belgium

8. Which tennis player was nicknamed 'the crocodile'?
   A: René Lacoste **B:** Henri Leconte **C:** Yannick Noah

9. How many times has Andy Murray won BBC Sports Personality of the Year?
   A: Zero **B:** Once **C:** Three times

10. Approximately 275,000 glasses of what drink are served at Wimbledon each year?
   A: Champagne **B:** Pimm's **C:** White wine

11. Spot the made-up tennis shot type lurking among the real shots below
   A: Lob **B:** Smash **C:** Bunt

12. What are the first names of the two Williams sisters?
   A: Neptune and Selena **B:** Venus and Serena
   C: Saturnia and Serafina

13. What is the name of Andy Murray's mum?
   A: Judy **B:** June **C:** Julie

14. Which singer famously entertained the crowd during a rainy day at Wimbledon in 1996?
   A: Geri Halliwell **B:** Cliff Richard **C:** Mick Jagger

15. The largest show court at Wimbledon is known as what?
   A: Centre Court **B:** Middle Court **C:** The Old Court

FIX THE FAULTS

Put these tennis legends' first names with their correct surnames:

1. Roger Graf
2. Rafael Sharapova
3. Andre Djokovic
4. Pete Navratilova
5. Novak Sampras
6. Martina King
7. Steffi Kournikova
8. Billie Jean Federer
9. Anna Agassi
10. Maria Nadal

TENNIS (MEDIUM)

ANAGRAMS

Unscramble the names of these former Wimbledon singles champions:

1. LORD RAVE
2. FAFF TIGERS
3. CHER STRIVE
4. HURRAH TEAS
5. REPEATS SPAM
6. RAINED SAGAS
7. ADARA FALLEN
8. DAY UNMARRY
9. EBBS ROCKIER
10. DEVAN POLYANDRIST
11. ANIMAL WIRELESS
12. ALUMNI SWIVELS
13. ARMANI INSIGHT
14. BEIJING KELLINA
15. ALAN AVIATOR VARMINT

ONE-TIME WIMBLEDON CHAMPIONS

Can you work out these one-time Wimbledon champions from the clues?

1. Australian who was engaged to Kim Clijsters.
2. Big-serving German who beat his compatriot in the 1991 final.
3. Only Dutch man to have won a Grand Slam tournament.
4. Las Vegas legend regarded as one of the best returners of all time.
5. Made headlines by climbing into the stands to celebrate his win in 1987.
6. She became the youngest Grand Slam singles champion of the 20th century in 1997.

7. Comforted by the Duchess of Kent after losing the final in 1993 before winning in 1998.
8. First Russian female player to top the rankings, which she did aged 18 in 2005.
9. Only Grand Slam chalked up by this popular Croat champion in 2001.
10. Champion in 2006 who went on to coach Andy Murray from 2014 to 2016.

MOST GRAND SLAMS

As at 12 July 2021, seven men have won 11 or more Grand Slam singles tournaments. Can you name them?

1. 1= (20 singles titles): ______________________________
2. 1= (20 singles titles): ______________________________
3. 1= (20 singles titles):______________________________
4. 4 (14 singles titles):______________________________
5. 5 (12 singles titles):______________________________
6. 6= (11 singles titles):______________________________
7. 6= (11 singles titles):______________________________

TRIVIA

1. Can you name and arrange the four Grand Slam tennis tournaments – the French Open, Wimbledon, Australian Open and the US Open – in calendar order?
2. Which is the only Grand Slam to use tiebreakers in every set of a singles match?
3. Who are the two largest show courts at the US Open named after?
4. In which city has the Australian Open been held since 1972?
5. Two of the Australian Open's show courts are named after former players. Name those legends!
6. Who did Andy Murray beat in straight sets to win the 2012 Olympic Gold medal?

7. Who married tennis legend Steffi Graf in 2001?
8. At which tournament is the Ladies Singles champion presented with the Venus Rosewater dish?
9. At which of the four Grand Slams were women and men first paid equal prize money?
10. In 1973, former Wimbledon and US Open Champion Bobby Riggs lost to which female tennis player in an internationally televised event dubbed the 'Battle of the Sexes'?
11. The longest tennis match of all time lasted over 11 hours and was played at Wimbledon in 2010 between French qualifier Nicolas Mahut and which seeded US player?
12. Which specialist doubles brothers won a total of 16 Grand Slam titles?
13. Which Australian pairing won 11 doubles titles together from 1992 to 2000?
14. Which British wheelchair player has, as at August 2021, won two Grand Slam singles tournaments, 16 Grand Slam doubles championships and a Paralympic Gold at Rio 2016?
15. Steffi Graf, Margaret Court and Serena Williams have won 69 Grand Slam singles titles between them. One has 24 titles, one has 23 and one has 22. Can you put them in the right order?

TENNIS (HARD)

NUMBER ONES

Since 1990, 20 players from 13 countries have held the men's number one ranking. Can you get them all?

1. AUSTRALIA x 2: __________ __________
2. AUSTRIA x 1: __________
3. BRAZIL x 1: __________
4. CHILE x 1: __________
5. CZECHOSLOVAKIA x 1: __________
6. GERMANY x 1: __________
7. GREAT BRITAIN x 1: __________
8. RUSSIA x 2: __________ __________
9. SERBIA x 1: __________
10. SPAIN x 3: __________ __________ __________
11. SWEDEN x 1: __________
12. SWITZERLAND x 1: __________
13. USA x 4: __________ __________ __________ __________

Since 1990, 23 players from 15 countries have held the women's number one ranking. Can you get them all from their initials, arranged in chronological order of the date they first reached the number one spot?

1. SG ____________________
2. MS ____________________
3. ASV ____________________
4. MH ____________________
5. LD ____________________
6. JC ____________________
7. VW ____________________
8. SW ____________________
9. KC ____________________
10. JH ____________________

11. AM ____________________ **18.** AK ____________________
12. MS ____________________ **19.** KP ____________________
13. AI ____________________ **20.** GM ____________________
14. JJ ____________________ **21.** SH ____________________
15. DS ____________________ **22.** NO ____________________
16. CW ____________________ **23.** AB ____________________
17. VA ____________________

BATTLING BRITS

1. Who was the last Brit before Andy Murray to reach the final at Wimbledon in the men's singles?
2. Who is the only Great British player to win all four major championships?
3. Which major tournament did Sue Barker win in 1976?
4. Who was the last Brit before Greg Rusedski to reach a major men's singles tournament final?
5. Virginia Wade was the last British woman to win a Wimbledon singles tournament, but which year did she win it?
6. Can you name the four players that Tim Henman heroically lost Wimbledon semi-finals to?

    ____________________ (1998)
    ____________________ (1999)
    ____________________ (2001)
    ____________________ (2002)

7. In which year did Great Britain last win the Davis Cup?

RECORD BREAKERS

1. Only four players in the history of men's and women's singles, two men and two women, have won the Golden Slam – all four major tournaments and the Olympic Gold Medal. Can you name them?

2. Which one of them achieved all of the above in one calendar year, and which year was it?
3. As at August 2021, who was the last unseeded woman to win a singles title at a major tournament?
4. Who retired in 2007, returned to the sport in 2009, and was granted a wildcard entry into the 2009 US Open before winning it?
5. Who was the first unseeded male singles player to win Wimbledon?
6. Who became the first wild-card entrant to win Wimbledon?
7. Which women's pair are unbeaten in 14 Grand Slam Doubles finals?
8. Who was the first African-American to win a Grand Slam singles final?
9. Which female tennis player has appeared in the most Grand Slam singles finals (34)?
10. Which country has won the most Davis Cups?

US SPORTS

(ANSWERS PAGE 296)

Last but not least, we've got a few questions from across the pond because we like to keep up to speed with the NFL, NBA and MLB. We are the world's biggest sports radio station after all! So step up to the plate and hit these last few out of the park!

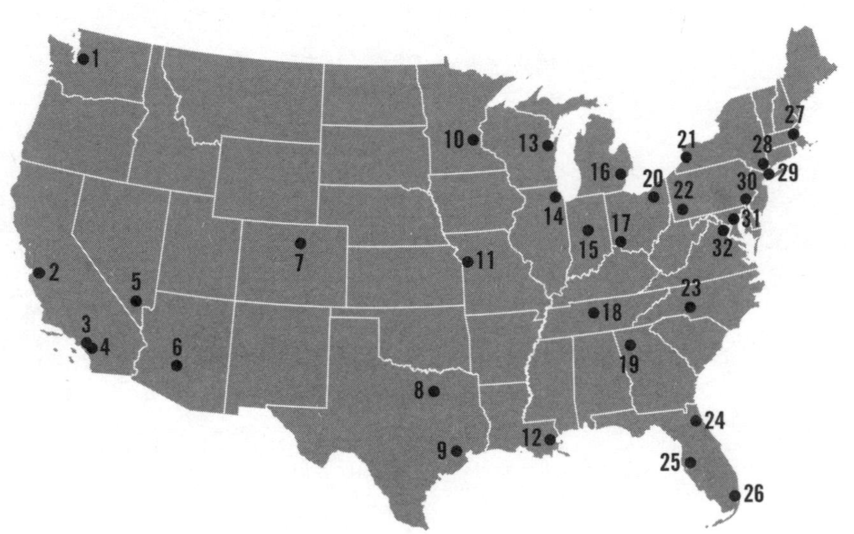
1
2
3
4
5
6
7
8
9
10
11
12
13
14
15
16
17
18
19
20
21
22
23
24
25
26
27
28
29
30
31
32

NFL

Can you match the 32 NFL teams to their locations in the US?

Arizona Cardinals
Atlanta Falcons
Baltimore Ravens
Buffalo Bills
Carolina Panthers
Chicago Bears
Cincinnati Bengals
Cleveland Browns
Dallas Cowboys
Denver Broncos
Detroit Lions
Green Bay Packers
Houston Texans
Indianapolis Colts
Jacksonville Jaguars
Kansas City Chiefs
Las Vegas Raiders
Los Angeles Chargers
Los Angeles Rams
Miami Dolphins
Minnesota Vikings
New England Patriots
New Orleans Saints
New York Giants
New York Jets
Philadelphia Eagles
Pittsburgh Steelers
San Francisco 49ers
Seattle Seahawks
Tampa Bay Buccaneers
Tennessee Titans
Washington Football Team

NBA

These NBA teams have got completely jumbled up. Can you match the correct first part of the team name with the second?

1. Atlanta Jazz
2. Boston 76ers
3. Brooklyn Clippers
4. Charlotte Knicks
5. Chicago Pistons
6. Cleveland Magic
7. Dallas Warriors
8. Denver Celtics
9. Detroit Hawks
10. Golden State Heat
11. Houston Pelicans
12. Indiana Spurs
13. Los Angeles Bulls
14. Los Angeles Hornets
15. Memphis Kings
16. Miami Lakers
17. Milwaukee Thunder
18. Minnesota Trail Blazers
19. New Orleans Suns
20. New York Pacers
21. Oklahoma City Cavaliers
22. Orlando Nuggets
23. Philadelphia Grizzlies
24. Phoenix Rockets
25. Portland Timberwolves
26. Sacramento Wizards
27. San Antonio Raptors
28. Toronto Nets
29. Utah Bucks
30. Washington Mavericks

MLB

Which cities do the following Major League Baseball teams belong to?

1. Angels
2. Astros
3. Athletics
4. Blue Jays
5. Braves
6. Brewers
7. Cardinals
8. Cubs
9. Diamondbacks
10. Dodgers
11. Giants
12. Indians
13. Mariners
14. Marlins
15. Mets
16. Nationals
17. Orioles
18. Padres
19. Phillies
20. Pirates
21. Rangers
22. Rays
23. Reds
24. Red Sox
25. Rockies
26. Royals
27. Tigers
28. Twins
29. White Sox
30. Yankees

ANSWERS

FOOTBALL (EASY)

(PAGE 5)

WHERE IN THE WORLD?

1. **B:** Italy
2. **A:** Japan
3. **C:** Germany
4. **B:** Brazil
5. **B:** Netherlands
6. **C:** South Korea
7. **B:** Greece

NATIONAL NICKNAMES

1. Les Bleus **France**
2. Gli Azzurri **Italy**
3. Oranje **Netherlands**
4. Y Dreigiau (The Dragons) **Wales**
5. Die Mannschaft **Germany**
6. All Whites **New Zealand**
7. Socceroos **Australia**
8. Reggae Boyz **Jamaica**
9. Stars & Stripes **USA**
10. The Pharaohs **Egypt**
11. Bafana Bafana **South Africa**
12. The Desert Warriors **Algeria**
13. Na Buachaillí i Nglas (The Boys in Green) **Ireland**
14. Ay Yıldızlılar (The Crescent-Stars) **Turkey**
15. The Three Lions **England**

KITS

1. **C:** White
2. **B:** Claret and Blue
3. **A:** Red (or Garnet) and Blue
4. **B:** White and Sky Blue
5. **A:** Red
6. **C:** Orange
7. **B:** Green

WAGS

1. Peter Crouch **Abbey Clancy**
2. David Beckham **Victoria Adams**
3. Jamie Redknapp **Louise Nurding**
4. Ashley Cole **Cheryl Tweedy**
5. Alex Oxlade-Chamberlain **Perrie Edwards**
6. Wayne Rooney **Coleen McLoughlin**
7. Gerard Piqué **Shakira**

WORLD CUP

1. **A:** 1986
2. **C:** Gordon Banks
3. **B:** Diego Simeone
4. **B:** Brazil
5. **A:** Wembley
6. **A:** Jules Rimet

RONALDO

1. **B:** Portugal
2. **A:** CR7
3. **C:** Madeira
4. **B:** Real Madrid
5. **B:** Wayne Rooney
6. **A:** Juventus
7. **B:** Nelson Mandela

MESSI

1. **A:** Argentina
2. **C:** Barcelona
3. **A:** Ballon d'Or
4. **C:** Adidas
5. **C:** $127 million
6. **B:** Diego Maradona
7. **A:** Tax Fraud

BECKHAM

1. **A:** 7
2. **A:** LA Galaxy
3. **B:** Greece
4. **A:** UNICEF UK
5. **C:** London
6. **B:** Sir Alex Ferguson
7. **C:** Argentina

WORLD'S RICHEST CLUBS

1. Barcelona
2. Real Madrid
3. Bayern Munich
4. Manchester United
5. Liverpool
6. Manchester City
7. Paris Saint-Germain
8. Chelsea
9. Tottenham Hotspur
10. Juventus
11. Arsenal
12. Borussia Dortmund
13. Atlético Madrid
14. Inter Milan
15. Zenit St Petersburg

CLUB NICKNAMES

1. Gunners **Arsenal**
2. Seagulls **Brighton**
3. Owls **Sheffield Wednesday**
4. Rams **Derby County**
5. Foxes **Leicester City**
6. Red Devils **Man Utd**
7. Reds **Liverpool**
8. Blades **Sheffield United**
9. Eagles **Crystal Palace**
10. Saints **Southampton**
11. Hammers **West Ham United**
12. Toffees **Everton**
13. Royals **Reading**
14. Magpies **Newcastle United**
15. Baggies **West Bromwich Albion**
16. Pompey **Portsmouth**
17. Gers **Rangers**
18. Bhoys **Celtic**
19. Wombles **AFC Wimbledon**
20. Bluebirds **Cardiff City**
21. Lions **Millwall**
22. Potters **Stoke City**

WORLD CUP-WINNING NATIONS

1. Spain
2. Italy
3. Germany
4. Brazil
5. Argentina
6. France

DERBIES

1. Celtic and Rangers
2. Norwich City and Ipswich Town
3. Arsenal and Tottenham Hotspur
4. Wolverhampton Wanderers and West Bromwich Albion
5. Liverpool and Everton
6. Crystal Palace and Brighton & Hove Albion
7. Newcastle United and Middlesbrough
8. Edinburgh

TRIVIA

1. **B:** David Beckham
2. **A:** 1966
3. **C:** Arsenal
4. **B:** Queens Park Rangers
5. **C:** Brazil
6. **A:** France
7. **C:** Premier League
8. **C:** Three
9. **A:** A penalty kick
10. **B:** Sir Alex Ferguson
11. **A:** West Germany
12. **C:** Croatia
13. **B:** Paul Gascoigne
14. **A:** Bayern Munich
15. **C:** Leicester City
16. **B:** 1960s
17. **B:** West Ham
18. **A:** Alan Shearer
19. **B:** 30 minutes
20. **A:** Harry Kane
21. **C:** Colombia
22. **C:** Liverpool
23. **B:** Gareth Southgate
24. **B:** Qatar
25. **A:** Europe
26. **C:** Wayne Rooney
27. **C:** Rangers
28. **A:** Gary Lineker
29. **B:** Neymar Jr
30. **C:** Harry Kane
31. **A:** The Three Tenors
32. **B:** Sven-Göran Eriksson
33. **C:** Northern Ireland
34. **B:** After Extra Time

FOOTBALL (MEDIUM)

(PAGE 17)

HARD MEN

1. Stuart Pearce
2. Terry Butcher
3. Neil Ruddock
4. Nigel de Jong
5. Thomas Gravesen
6. Vincent Kompany
7. Vinnie Jones
8. Duncan Ferguson
9. Joe Jordan
10. Ron Harris
11. Mick Harford
12. Patrick Vieira
13. Roy Keane
14. Ryan Shawcross
15. Franz Beckenbauer

GAFFERS' NICKNAMES

1. The Special One **José Mourinho**
2. The Tinker Man **Claudio Ranieri**
3. The Wally with the Brolly **Steve McClaren**
4. The Godfather **Antonio Conte**
5. Le Professeur **Arsène Wenger**
6. The Exceptional One **Pep Guardiola**

DEADLINE DAY DEALS

1. Carlos Tevez and Javier Mascherano
2. Ashley Cole
3. Claude Makélélé
4. Wayne Rooney
5. Peter Crouch
6. Fernando Torres
7. Luis Suárez
8. Harry Redknapp

WHERE ARE YER?

1. Newcastle United
2. Burnley
3. Leeds United
4. Liverpool
5. Everton
6. Manchester United
7. Manchester City
8. Norwich City
9. Wolverhampton Wanderers
10. Aston Villa
11. Leicester City
12. Watford
13. Southampton
14. Brighton & Hove Albion
15. Tottenham Hotspur
16. Arsenal
17. West Ham United
18. Brentford
19. Chelsea
20. Crystal Palace

WONDER GOALS

1. **Michael Owen** (scoring England's second against Argentina in the round of 16 at the 1998 World Cup in France)
2. **Diego Maradona** (scoring the second of his two goals in the World Cup quarter-final of 1986 between England and Argentina)
3. **Marco van Basten** (scoring the second of the Netherlands' two goals in the final of Euro 1988 against the Soviet Union)
4. **Dennis Bergkamp** (scoring against Argentina in the quarter-finals of the 1998 World Cup)
5. **Zlatan Ibrahimović** (scoring his fourth goal against England in a 2012 friendly)
6. **Carlos Alberto** (scoring the fourth goal in Brazil's 4–1 demolition of Italy in the 1970 World Cup Final)

MATCH THE CLUB TO THE COUNTRY

1. Maccabi Haifa **Israel**
2. Heerenveen **Netherlands**
3. Trabzonspor **Turkey**
4. Red Star Belgrade **Serbia**
5. Genk **Belgium**
6. Young Boys **Switzerland**
7. FC Copenhagen **Denmark**
8. CFR Cluj **Romania**
9. Helsingborg **Sweden**
10. Sturm Graz **Austria**
11. Sparta Prague **Czech Republic**
12. Rubin Kazan **Russia**
13. Shakhtar Donetsk **Ukraine**
14. Molde **Norway**
15. Dinamo Zagreb **Croatia**
16. Legia Warsaw **Poland**
17. Levski Sofia **Bulgaria**
18. Debrecen **Hungary**
19. Maribor **Slovenia**
20. Qarabağ **Azerbaijan**
21. BATE Borisov **Belarus**
22. Astana **Kazakhstan**
23. Panathinaikos **Greece**
24. Braga **Portugal**
25. 1899 Hoffenheim **Germany**
26. Celta Vigo **Spain**
27. Lens **France**
28. Atalanta **Italy**

CHANTS FROM THE TERRACES

1. Millwall
2. Leeds United
3. Manchester City
4. West Ham United
5. (Olivier) Giroud
6. Peter Crouch
7. (Bobby) Zamora
8. Newcastle United

PREMIER LEAGUE HAT-TRICKS

PLAYER	Number of hat-tricks	First hat-trick	Most recent hat-trick	Club(s) scored for
Sergio Agüero	12	10/9/2011	12/01/2020	Man City
Alan Shearer	11	23/10/1993	19/09/1999	Blackburn Rovers, Newcastle Utd
Robbie Fowler	9	30/10/1993	26/12/2001	Liverpool, Leeds Utd
Thierry Henry	8	26/12/2000	07/05/2006	Arsenal
Harry Kane	8	21/03/2015	26/12/2017	Tottenham Hotspur
Michael Owen	8	14/02/1998	17/12/2005	Liverpool, Newcastle Utd
Wayne Rooney	7	28/10/2006	29/11/2017	Man Utd, Everton
Luis Suárez	6	28/04/2012	22/03/2014	Liverpool
Dimitar Berbatov	5	29/12/2007	26/12/2011	Tottenham Hotspur, Man Utd
Robin van Persie	5	22/01/2011	22/04/2013	Arsenal, Man Utd
Ruud van Nistelrooy	5	22/12/2001	27/09/2003	Man Utd
Andy Cole	5	21/11/1993	30/08/1999	Newcastle Utd, Man Utd
Ian Wright	5	05/03/1994	13/12/1997	Arsenal

FIVE FAMOUS FREE KICKS

1. **Ronaldinho**, who made it 2–1 to Brazil in heartbreaking fashion (for England fans, anyway), sending England out of the World Cup.
2. **Roberto Carlos**, scoring a free kick which began its trajectory closer to the corner flag than the goal before bending in with incredible pace and power.
3. **David Beckham**, who raised the roof by securing England's qualification to the 2002 World Cup.
4. **Cristiano Ronaldo** scoring for Manchester United in the Premier League in January 2008.
5. Southampton's **Matt Le Tissier** with a moment of magic in a 1994 Premier League match that inspired schoolboys everywhere.

WHO'S HE ON ABOUT?

1. Kylian Mbappé
2. Johan Cruyff
3. Sir Bobby Charlton
4. Neymar Jr
5. Ronaldinho
6. Thierry Henry
7. Zinedine Zidane
8. Diego Maradona
9. Gianluigi Buffon
10. Andrés Iniesta
11. Roberto Carlos
12. Pelé
13. Alessandro Del Piero
14. Cristiano Ronaldo
15. Franz Beckenbauer

PLAYERS' NICKNAMES

1. Baby-faced Assassin **Ole Gunnar Solskjær**
2. The Guv'nor **Paul Ince**
3. Non-flying Dutchman **Dennis Bergkamp**
4. Chicharito (Little Pea) **Javier Hernández**
5. Il Divino Codino (The Divine Ponytail) **Roberto Baggio**
6. Sick Note **Darren Anderton**
7. Psycho **Stuart Pearce**
8. Golden Balls **David Beckham**
9. The Fifth Beatle **George Best**
10. Mr Arsenal **Tony Adams**
11. Romford Pelé **Ray Parlour**

MASCOTS

1. Arsenal **Gunnersaurus**
2. Aston Villa **Hercules the Lion**
3. Brentford **Buzz and Buzzette**
4. Brighton & Hove Albion **Gully the Seagull**
5. Burnley **Bertie Bee**
6. Chelsea **Stamford and Bridget the Lion**
7. Crystal Palace **Pete the Eagle**
8. Leeds United **Kop Cat**
9. Leicester City **Filbert Fox**
10. Liverpool **Mighty Red**
11. Manchester City **Moonchester**
12. Manchester Utd **Fred the Red**
13. Newcastle United **Monty Magpie**
14. Norwich City **Captain Canary**
15. Southampton **Sammy Saint**
16. Tottenham Hotspur **Chirpy**
17. Watford **Harry the Hornet**
18. West Ham United **Hammerhead**
19. Wolverhampton Wanderers **Wolfie and Wendy**

POST-MATCH MAGIC

1. Ron Atkinson
2. Sir Alex Ferguson
3. Arsène Wenger
4. Claudio Ranieri
5. José Mourinho
6. Kevin Keegan
7. Harry Redknapp
8. Ian Holloway
9. Bill Shankly
10. Brian Clough

SAY WHAT?

1. Eric Cantona
2. Zlatan Ibrahimović
3. Wayne Rooney
4. George Best
5. Mario Balotelli
6. John Barnes
7. Peter Crouch
8. Paul Gascoigne
9. Michael Owen
10. Ian Rush

MOST CAPPED ENGLAND PLAYERS

1. Peter Shilton
2. Wayne Rooney
3. David Beckham
4. Steven Gerrard
5. Bobby Moore
6. Ashley Cole
7. Bobby Charlton
8. Frank Lampard
9. Billy Wright
10. Bryan Robson

ENGLAND'S PENALTY PAIN

1. Stuart Pearce and Chris Waddle
2. Gareth Southgate
3. Paul Ince and David Batty
4. David Beckham and Darius Vassell
5. Frank Lampard, Steven Gerrard and Jamie Carragher
6. Ashley Young and Ashley Cole
7. Alan Shearer, David Platt, Stuart Pearce and Paul Gascoigne

WHO ARE YER?

1. Portsmouth **Fratton Park**
2. West Bromwich Albion **The Hawthorns**
3. Charlton Athletic **The Valley**
4. Coventry City **Ricoh Arena**
5. Millwall **The Den**
6. Norwich City **Carrow Road**
7. Sunderland **Stadium of Light**
8. Ipswich Town **Portman Road**
9. Luton **Kenilworth Road**
10. Reading **Madejski Stadium**
11. Watford **Vicarage Road**
12. Preston North End **Deepdale**
13. Notts County **Meadow Lane**
14. Middlesbrough **Riverside Stadium**
15. QPR **Loftus Road**
16. Bournemouth **Vitality Stadium**

ANAGRAMS

1. LATIN MINER **INTER MILAN**
2. OIL PAN **NAPOLI**
3. I ZOLA **LAZIO**
4. SEED UNI **UDINESE**
5. RADIO SPAM **SAMPDORIA**
6. ANOINT FIRE **FIORENTINA**
7. NO RIOT **TORINO**
8. A RAMP **PARMA**
9. ANAL MIC **AC MILAN**
10. JET SUN UV **JUVENTUS**

Untangle the names of the La Liga teams:

1. COBRA LANE **BARCELONA**
2. ADMIRAL DRE **REAL MADRID**
3. LIL VASE **SEVILLA**
4. LIBERATES **REAL BETIS**
5. NICE LAVA **VALENCIA**
6. LARVAL LIE **VILLAREAL**
7. DICTATOR MAILED **ATLÉTICO MADRID**
8. ETHICAL BOBTAIL **ATHLETIC BILBAO**
9. ARCADE SOILED **REAL SOCIEDAD**
10. SO SAUNA **OSASUNA**

OWN GOALS AND GAFFES

1. A beach ball
2. Lee Dixon
3. Richard Dunne
4. Ronnie Rosenthal
5. Nwankwo Kanu

PREMIER LEAGUE RED CARDS

1. Richard Dunne
2. Duncan Ferguson
3. Patrick Vieira
4. Lee Cattermole
5. Vinnie Jones
6. Roy Keane
7. Alan Smith

IT'S NOT A QUESTION OF SPORT

PETE / ER / SSH / MICE / COOL
PETER SCHMEICHEL

DAY / VID / GIN / OLA
DAVID GINOLA

RAY / WIL / KIN / S
RAY WILKINS

TROY / DEAN / EY
TROY DEENEY

BURN / HARD / DOE / SILVER
BERNARDO SILVA

FILL / FOE / DEN
PHIL FODEN

KIR / ANT / RIP / PIER
KIERAN TRIPPIER

JESS / SEA / LING / GUARD
JESSE LINGARD

MAY / SON / MOUNT
MASON MOUNT

SIR / GEO / RAM / MOSS
SERGIO RAMOS

LION / HELL / MESSI
LIONEL MESSI

ROW / BUR / TOW / FIRM / MEAN / OH
ROBERTO FIRMINO

ROB / BIN / VAN / PURR / SEE
ROBIN VAN PERSIE

MEMPHIS / TO PAY
MEMPHIS DEPAY

LOO / CAR / MOD / RICH
LUKA MODRIĆ

EDEN / HAZARD
EDEN HAZARD

FILLY / YPRES / COOT / TEEN / YO
PHILIPPE COUTINHO

MO / HAM / MED / CELLAR
MOHAMED SALAH

DIE / GO / MA / RAD / DONNA
DIEGO MARADONA

VERGE / JILL / VAN / DYKE
VIRGIL VAN DIJK

PREMIER LEAGUE CLUBS

1. Arsenal
2. Aston Villa
3. Barnsley
4. Birmingham City
5. Blackburn Rovers
6. Blackpool
7. Bolton Wanderers
8. Bournemouth
9. Bradford City
10. Brentford
11. Brighton & Hove Albion
12. Burnley
13. Cardiff City
14. Charlton Athletic
15. Chelsea
16. Coventry
17. Crystal Palace
18. Derby County
19. Everton
20. Fulham
21. Huddersfield Town
22. Hull City
23. Ipswich Town
24. Leeds United
25. Leicester City
26. Liverpool
27. Manchester City
28. Manchester United
29. Middlesbrough
30. Newcastle United
31. Norwich City
32. Nottingham Forest
33. Oldham Athletic
34. Portsmouth
35. Queens Park Rangers
36. Reading

37. Sheffield United
38. Sheffield Wednesday
39. Southampton
40. Stoke City
41. Sunderland
42. Swansea City
43. Swindon Town
44. Tottenham Hotspur
45. Watford
46. West Bromwich Albion
47. West Ham United
48. Wigan Athletic
49. Wimbledon
50. Wolverhampton Wanderers

SCOTTISH PREMIER LEAGUE

1. Aberdeen
2. Celtic
3. Dundee
4. Dundee United
5. Hamilton Academical
6. Hearts
7. Hibernian
8. Inverness Caledonian Thistle
9. Kilmarnock
10. Livingston
11. Motherwell
12. Partick Thistle
13. Rangers
14. Ross County
15. St Johnstone
16. St Mirren

TRIVIA

1. 23
2. Sepp Blatter
3. Manchester City
4. Leeds United
5. Milton Keynes
6. Green and gold, harking back to the colours worn by Newton Heath, the club founded in 1878 that became Manchester Utd in 1902
7. Delia Smith
8. Elton John
9. West Ham
10. AC Milan
11. Ole Gunnar Solskjaer (Ole with a Brolly)
12. Rivaldo

FOOTBALL (HARD)

(PAGE 40)

FOOTBALL LEAGUE AND NON-LEAGUE

1. Nicky Butt, Ryan Giggs, Gary Neville, Phil Neville and Paul Scholes
2. Eric Morecambe
3. Rotherham United
4. Louis Tomlinson
5. Fleetwood Town
6. AFC Barnet, Blackpool, Hull City and Wolverhampton Wanderers

EFL AND PREMIER LEAGUE CLUBS

1. Bradford City
2. Swindon Town
3. Fleetwood Town
4. Millwall
5. AFC Wimbledon (78 league matches between 26 February 2003 and 27 November 2004)
6. West Ham United
7. Leyton Orient
8. Derby County
9. Plymouth Argyle
10. Norwich City

EFL CLUBS

1. Brighton & Hove, West Bromwich, Burton
2. Charlton, Oldham, Wigan
3. Birmingham, Bradford, Bristol, Cardiff, Coventry, Exeter, Hull, Leicester, Lincoln, Manchester, Norwich, Salford, Stoke, Swansea

4. Derby, Newport
5. Blackburn, Bristol, Doncaster, Forest Green, Tranmere
6. Cheltenham, Crawley, Fleetwood, Harrogate, Huddersfield, Ipswich, Luton, Mansfield, Northampton, Shrewsbury, Swindon
7. Cambridge, Carlisle, Colchester, Hartlepool, Leeds, Manchester, Newcastle, Oxford, Peterborough, Rotherham, Scunthorpe, Sheffield, Sutton, West Ham
8. Bolton, Wycombe, Wolverhampton

FIRST FOOTBALL LEAGUE CLUBS

1. Accrington
2. Aston Villa
3. Blackburn Rovers
4. Bolton Wanderers
5. Burnley
6. Derby County
7. Everton
8. Notts County
9. Preston North End
10. Stoke
11. West Bromwich Albion
12. Wolverhampton Wanderers

UNBELIEVABLE SCENES

1. Portugal and the Netherlands
2. Harald Schumacher
3. John Terry (who offered his hand) and Wayne Bridge (who didn't) following allegations that Terry had an affair with Bridge's partner, Vanessa Perroncel
4. Marco Materazzi

HALFWAY LINE AND BEYOND

1. Xabi Alonso
2. Wayne Rooney
3. Maynor Figueroa
4. David Beckham
5. Tim Howard
6. Asmir Begović
7. Charlie Adam

HISTORY MAKERS

1. Johan Cruyff
2. Panenka, named after Antonín Panenka
3. Mexico's Cuauhtémoc Blanco
4. René Higuita
5. Vinnie Jones
6. Denis Law
7. Trevor Francis
8. Jack Grealish, who joined Manchester City from Aston Villa for a reported £100 million on 5 August 2021
9. Kepa Arrizabalaga, who was bought by Chelsea for €80 million
10. Kylian Mbappé
11. Edwin van der Sar
12. José Luis Chilavert (Paraguay)

FILL IN THE TEAMS

England starting line-up for the Euro 96 semi-final against Germany:

GK David Seaman
CB Stuart Pearce
CB Tony Adams
CB Gareth Southgate
CM David Platt
CM Paul Ince
CM Paul Gascoigne
WB Steve McManaman
WB Darren Anderton
F Teddy Sheringham
F Alan Shearer

Arsenal's most-used starters that comprised the 'Invincibles' team of 2003–04:

GK Jens Lehmann
LB Ashley Cole
CB Sol Campbell
CB Kolo Touré
RB Lauren
CM Patrick Vieira
CM Gilberto Silva
LM Robert Pires
RM Freddie Ljungberg
F Dennis Bergkamp
F Thierry Henry

2008 Champions League Final starting XIs:

Chelsea

GK Petr Čech
LB Ashley Cole
CB Ricardo Carvalho
CB John Terry
RB Michael Essien
DM Claude Makélélé
CM Michael Ballack
CM Frank Lampard
LW Joe Cole
RW Florent Malouda
F Didier Drogba

Man Utd

GK Edwin van der Sar
LB Patrice Evra
CB Rio Ferdinand
CB Nemanja Vidić
RB Wes Brown
CM Paul Scholes
CM Michael Carrick
LM Cristiano Ronaldo
RM Owen Hargreaves
F Carlos Tevez
F Wayne Rooney

Man City line-up for the last game of the 2011–2012 Premier League season:

GK Joe Hart
LB Gaël Clichy
CB Joleon Lescott
CB Vincent Kompany
RB Pablo Zabaleta
CM Gareth Barry
CM Yaya Touré
LM Samir Nasri
RM David Silva
F Sergio Agüero
F Carlos Tevez

SHIRT SPONSORS

First season of the Premier League:

1. Arsenal **JVC**
2. Aston Villa **Mita Copiers**
3. Blackburn Rovers **McEwan's Lager**
4. Chelsea **Commodore**
5. Coventry City **Peugeot**
6. Crystal Palace **Tulip Computers**
7. Everton **NEC**
8. Ipswich Town **Fisons**
9. Leeds United **Admiral Sportswear**
10. Liverpool **Carlsberg**
11. Man City **Brother**
12. Man Utd **Sharp**
13. Middlesbrough **ICI**
14. Nottingham Forest **Labatt's**
15. Norwich City **Norwich and Peterborough Building Society**
16. Oldham Athletic **J-D Sports**
17. QPR **Classic FM**
18. Sheffield United **Laver**
19. Sheffield Wednesday **Sanderson**
20. Southampton **Draper Tools**
21. Tottenham Hotspur **Holsten**
22. Wimbledon **No shirt sponsor**

Turn of the millennium:

1. Arsenal **Dreamcast**
2. Aston Villa **LDV Vans**
3. Bradford **JCT600**
4. Chelsea **Autoglass**
5. Coventry City **Subaru**
6. Derby County **EDC**
7. Everton **One2One**
8. Leeds United **Packard Bell**
9. Leicester City **Walkers Crisps**
10. Liverpool **Carlsberg**
11. Man Utd **Sharp**
12. Middlesbrough **BT Cellnet**
13. Newcastle United **Newcastle Brown Ale**
14. Sheffield Wednesday **Sanderson**
15. Southampton **Friends Provident**
16. Sunderland **Reg Vardy**
17. Tottenham Hotspur **Holsten**
18. Watford **Phones4U**
19. West Ham United **Dr Martens**
20. Wimbledon **Tiny**

CHARISMATIC CHAIRMEN AND OWNERS

1. Sam Hammam
2. Vincent Tan
3. Mike Ashley
4. Simon Jordan
5. Ken Bates
6. Alan Sugar

LATIN MOTTOS

1. *Arte et Labore* (By Skill and Labour) **Blackburn**
2. *Audere est Facere* (To Dare is to Do) **Tottenham Hotspur**
3. *Nil Satis Nisi Optimum* (Nothing but the Best Is Good Enough) **Everton**
4. *Consilio et Anamis* (Intelligence and Courage) **Sheffield Wednesday**
5. *Vincit Omnia Industria* (Hard Work Conquers All) **Bury**
6. *Consectatio Excellentiae* (In Pursuit of Excellence) **Sunderland**
7. *Confidemus* (We Trust) **Kilmarnock**

8. *Superbia in Proelio* (Pride in Battle) **Manchester City**
9. *Victoria Concordia Crescit* (Victory through Harmony) **Arsenal**
10. *Floreat Salopia* (May Shropshire Flourish) **Shrewsbury**

MATCH THE STADIUM TO THE CLUB

1. Camp Nou **Barcelona**
2. Estadio Santiago Bernabeu **Real Madrid**
3. Signal Iduna Park **Borussia Dortmund**
4. San Siro **AC Milan/ Inter**
5. Allianz Arena **Bayern Munich**
6. Stadio Olimpico **Roma/ Lazio**
7. Metropolitano Stadium **Atlético Madrid**
8. Stade Vélodrome **Marseille**
9. Estádio da Luz **Benfica**
10. Johan Cruyff Arena **Ajax**
11. Stadio Diego Armando Maradona **Napoli**
12. La Bombonera **Boca Juniors**
13. Estádio do Dragão **Porto**
14. Mestalla Stadium **Valencia**
15. Red Bull Arena **RB Leipzig**
16. Türk Telekom Stadium **Galatasaray**
17. NSC Olimpiyskiy **FC Shakhtar Donetsk**
18. Rajko Mitić Stadium **Red Star Belgrade**
19. BayArena **Bayer Leverkusen**
20. Parc des Princes **Paris Saint-Germain**

WOMEN'S FOOTBALL

1. Lucy Bronze
2. USA
3. Megan Rapinoe
4. Phil Neville
5. Marta
6. Four (1991, 1999, 2015, 2019)
7. Alex Morgan
8. Lyon
9. Alex Scott
10. Steph Houghton

SIX OF THE BEST ONE-CLUB FOOTBALLERS

1. Ryan Giggs
2. Francesco Totti
3. Paolo Maldini
4. Jack Charlton
5. Carles Puyol
6. John Terry

MULTI-CLUB LEGENDS

1. James Milner: Leeds United, Newcastle United, Aston Villa, Manchester City, Liverpool
2. Emile Heskey: Leicester, Liverpool, Birmingham City, Wigan Athletic, Aston Villa
3. Robbie Keane: Coventry City, Leeds United, Tottenham Hotspur, Liverpool, West Ham United (on loan), Aston Villa (on loan)
4. Peter Crouch: Aston Villa, Southampton, Liverpool, Portsmouth, Tottenham Hotspur, Stoke City, Burnley
5. Craig Bellamy: Coventry City, Newcastle United, Blackburn Rovers, Liverpool, West Ham United, Manchester City, Cardiff City

WORLD CUP

1. Geoff Hurst and Eusebio
2. Pelé
3. Gonzalo Higuaín
4. Harry Kane and Cristiano Ronaldo
5. North Korea
6. Lothar Matthäus with 25 appearances between 1982 and 1998
7. Gabriel Batistuta (in 1994 and 1998)
8. Canada, Mexico and the USA
9. The vuvuzela
10. Ghana
11. Giorgio Chiellini
12. He pooed himself after suffering from a stomach bug
13. Frank Lampard
14. Diego Maradona
15. Thierry Henry
16. Peter Shilton
17. Steven Gerrard; Jermain Defoe; Matthew Upson; Daniel Sturridge; Wayne Rooney; Harry Kane; John Stones; Jesse Lingard; Harry Maguire; Dele Alli; Kieran Trippier
18. Ray Wilkins (1986, England v Morocco); David Beckham (1998, England v Argentina); Wayne Rooney (2006, England v Portugal)
19. Rigobert Song (Cameroon v Brazil, 1994; Cameroon v Chile, 1998); Zinedine Zidane (France v Saudi Arabia, 1998; France v Italy, 2006)
20. Tim Cahill (Australia v Germany); Harry Kewell (Australia v Ghana)

EUROS

1. 1960
2. Yugoslavia (beat England 1–0)
3. Marco van Basten
4. Michel Platini
5. Czech Republic
6. Alan Shearer (with five goals)
7. David Seaman, Steve McManaman, Paul Gascoigne, Alan Shearer
8. Spain (2008 and 2012)
9. *Goalkeeper:* Gianluigi Buffon, *Defender:* Paolo Maldini, *Defender:* Franz Beckenbauer, *Defender:* Carles Puyol, *Defender:* Philipp Lahm, *Midfielder:* Andrés Iniesta, *Midfielder:* Andrea Pirlo, *Midfielder:* Zinedine Zidane, *Forward:* Cristiano Ronaldo, *Forward:* Thierry Henry, *Forward:* Marco van Basten
10. Antoine Griezmann
11. Joe Allen and Aaron Ramsey
12. Eric Dier (v Russia), Jamie Vardy (v Wales), Daniel Sturridge (v Wales), Wayne Rooney (v Iceland)
13. Turkey; Denmark; Netherlands; England; Spain; Hungary; Italy; Finland; Ukraine; Croatia; Sweden; Portugal; Wales; Belgium; Austria; Scotland; Poland; France; Switzerland; Russia; North Macedonia; Czech Republic; Slovakia; Germany
14. Cristiano Ronaldo and Patrik Schick
15. Billy Gilmour
16. Marko Arnautović
17. Coca-Cola
18. Kasper Schmeichel
19. 34
20. Jordan Pickford, John Stones, Declan Rice, Kalvin Phillips, Harry Kane and Raheem Sterling
21. Conor Coady, Ben Chilwell and Ben White
22. Jadon Sancho
23. Michael Owen (v Argentina, World Cup 1998); Wayne Rooney (v Portugal, Euro 2004); Bukayo Saka (v Germany, Euro 2020)
24. Five
25. Kieran Trippier
26. Jordan Henderson
27. Peter Schmeichel

CHAMPIONS LEAGUE AND EUROPEAN CUP

1. Aston Villa
2. Celtic, Benfica, Porto, Red Star Belgrade and Steaua Bucureşti
3. Real Madrid (between 1956 and 1960)
4. Arsenal (losing 2–1 to Barcelona in 2006), Liverpool (losing 2–1 to Milan in 2007), Chelsea (losing on penalties to Man Utd in 2008) and Manchester United (losing 2–0 to Barcelona in 2009)
5. Pep Guardiola (aged 38 years and 129 days with Barcelona in 2009)
6. Istanbul
7. Arsenal, Blackburn Rovers, Chelsea, Everton (who were knocked out in the third qualifying round by Villareal in 2005), Leeds United, Leicester City, Liverpool, Manchester City, Manchester United, Newcastle United, Tottenham Hotspur
8. Vicente del Bosque (Champions League in 2000 and 2002 with Real Madrid, World Cup in 2010 with Spain, European Championships in 2012 with Spain)
9. Teddy Sheringham, 1999, Bayern Munich v Man Utd; Steve McManaman, 2000, Real Madrid v Valencia; Steven Gerrard, 2005, AC Milan v Liverpool; Sol Campbell, 2006, Arsenal v Barcelona; Frank Lampard, 2008, Chelsea v Man Utd; Wayne Rooney, 2011, Barcelona v Man Utd

ALL-TIME CHAMPIONS LEAGUE/EUROPEAN CUP SCORERS

Rank	Player	Nationality	Goals	Years	Club(s) (Goals)
1	**Cristiano Ronaldo**	**Portuguese**	134	2003–	**Manchester United (15)** Real Madrid (105) **Juventus (14)**
2	**Lionel Messi**	**Argentinian**	120	2005–	Barcelona
3	**Robert Lewandowski**	Polish	73	2011–	Borussia Dortmund (17) **Bayern Munich (56)**
4=	Raúl	**Spanish**	71	1995–2011	**Real Madrid (66)** Schalke 04 (5)
4=	**Karim Benzema**	French	71	2006–	Lyon (12) Real Madrid (59)
6	**Ruud van Nistelrooy**	Dutch	56	1998–2009	**PSV Eindhoven (8)** Manchester United (35) **Real Madrid (13)**
7	**Thierry Henry**	**French**	50	1997–2012	Monaco (7) Arsenal (35) **Barcelona (8)**
8	**Alfredo Di Stéfano**	Argentinian	49	1955–1964	Real Madrid

UEFA CUP/EUROPA LEAGUE

1. 11
2. Sevilla (six wins)
3. Arsenal
4. Ipswich Town
5. Henrik Larsson
6. Tottenham Hotspur
7. Steven Gerrard, Robbie Fowler, Daniel Sturridge

FA CUP

1. Dave Beasant (Wimbledon goalkeeper saved a penalty from Liverpool's John Aldridge in 1988)
2. Arsène Wenger (7)
3. Ashley Cole
4. Wigan Athletic
5. Wrexham
6. Nwankwo Kanu and Marc Overmars
7. Steven Gerrard
8. Stanley Matthews
9. Kevin Moran (Man Utd v Everton, 1985); José Antonio Reyes (Arsenal v Man Utd, 2005); Pablo Zabaleta (Man City v Wigan, 2013); Chris Smalling (Man Utd v Crystal Palace, 2016); Victor Moses (Chelsea v Arsenal, 2017); Mateo Kovačić (Chelsea v Arsenal, 2020)

ENGLISH LEAGUE CUP

1. 1982–86: Milk Cup (sponsored by the Milk Marketing Board); 1987–90: Littlewoods Challenge Cup; 1991–92: Rumbelows Cup; 1993–98: Coca-Cola Cup; 1999–2003: Worthington Cup; 2004–12: Carling Cup; 2013–16: Capital One; 2019–present: Carabao Cup
2. Sergio Agüero, David Silva and Fernandinho

SERIE A

1. Juventus
2. Rossoneri (red/black) = AC Milan; Nerazzurri (black/blue) = Inter; Bianconeri (white/black) = Juventus; Viola (purple) = Fiorentina; Giallorossi (yellow/red) = Roma; Azzurri (blue) = Napoli; Gialloblu (yellow/blue) = Parma; Biancocelesti (white/sky blue) = Lazio
3. Bari
4. Lazio
5. Inter

LA LIGA

1. Athletic Bilbao
2. Valencia in 2004
3. Sevilla
4. Lionel Messi
5. Deportivo La Coruña
6. Alfredo Di Stéfano
7. Sergio Ramos (45)

GALÁCTICOS

1. Luís Figo
2. Zinedine Zidane
3. Ronaldo
4. David Beckham
5. Michael Owen
6. Robinho
7. Sergio Ramos

USA, USA!

1. Landon Donovan and Clint Dempsey (tied on 57 goals)
2. Inter Miami CF
3. New York Red Bulls
4. David Villa
5. The Rose Bowl, Pasadena
6. 1–1 (Gerrard and Dempsey scoring)
7. Jürgen Klinsmann

DERBIES

1. Bayern Munich and Borussia Dortmund
2. Roma and Lazio
3. Barcelona and Real Madrid
4. Porto and Benfica
5. Corinthians and Palmeiras
6. Ajax and Feyenoord
7. Galatasaray and Fenerbahçe
8. Boca Juniors and River Plate

FORMERLY KNOWN AS

1. Dial Square **Arsenal**
2. Small Heath Alliance **Birmingham City**
3. St Luke's **Wolverhampton Wanderers**
4. St Domingo **Everton**
5. Newton Heath Lancashire and Yorkshire Railway **Manchester United**
6. Thames Ironworks **West Ham United**
7. St Mark's (West Gorton) **Manchester City**

ANAGRAMS

England captains:

1. BE BOY BROOM **BOBBY MOORE**
2. AKIN KNEE VEG **KEVIN KEEGAN**
3. LEAKY RINGER **GARY LINEKER**
4. ARSENAL HARE **ALAN SHEARER**
5. DARTS REVENGER **STEVEN GERRARD**
6. NARKY RHEAR **HARRY KANE**
7. MONDAYS TA **TONY ADAMS**
8. ABSORB RONNY **BRYAN ROBSON**
9. INFRARED ODIN **RIO FERDINAND**
10. CAPTURE STARE **STUART PEARCE**

Football grounds:

1. FAN IDLE **ANFIELD**
2. RUTH SPARKLES **SELHURST PARK**
3. FAT FORD LORD **OLD TRAFFORD**
4. RECONTACT VEGA **CRAVEN COTTAGE**
5. LADDER LOAN **ELLAND ROAD**
6. DROOPING OAKS **GOODISON PARK**
7. SHEATH THROWN **THE HAWTHORNS**
8. GAMBITS REDFORD **STAMFORD BRIDGE**
9. FUR MOTOR **TURF MOOR**

10. LEO UNMIX **MOLINEUX**
11. BLUR HIGH LOOS **HILLSBOROUGH**
12. OAK POWDER **EWOOD PARK**
13. BELLMAN LARA **BRAMALL LANE**
14. COWARD ROAR **CARROW ROAD**
15. HOGAN TEATS **ASHTON GATE**

Bundesliga clubs:

1. BUN MACHINERY **BAYERN MUNICH**
2. TROUBADOURS MINDS **BORUSSIA DORTMUND**
3. GLIB PRIZE **RB LEIPZIG**
4. THANK CURRENT TARIFF **EINTRACHT FRANKFURT**
5. REVERSELY UNBAKE **BAYER LEVERKUSEN**
6. ALAMO BUNCHING CHESSBOARD **BORUSSIA MÖNCHENGLADBACH**
7. BRETHREN HAIL **HERTHA BERLIN**
8. BUTT GRAFTS TV **VFB STUTTGART**
9. BREWER MENDER **WERDER BREMEN**
10. CUBS FUR GAG **FC AUGSBURG**

COMMENTARY GOLD

1. 'The Crazy Gang have beaten the culture club' **John Motson**
2. 'Football is a simple game; 22 men chase a ball for 90 minutes and at the end, the Germans win' **Gary Lineker**
3. 'You can't win anything with kids' **Alan Hansen**
4. 'And Solskjaer has won it!' **Clive Tyldesley**
5. 'Aguerooooooooooooooooo!!!! I swear you'll never see anything like this ever again!' **Martin Tyler**
6. 'DENNIS BERGKAMP, DENNIS BERGKAMP, DENNIS BERGKAMP, DENNIS BERGKAMP, DENNIS BERGKAMP!!!!!!!!!!!' **Jack van Gelder**
7. 'Pelé! What a save! Gordon Banks!' **David Coleman**

8. 'Oh, you beauty! What a hit, son. What a hit' **Andy Gray**
9. 'And you have to say that is magnificent' **Barry Davies**
10. 'The Dutch weren't ready, the defence wasn't steady, and there was good old Teddy!' **Jonathan Pearce**

TRIVIA

1. 2003
2. 2005
3. Score in a penalty shoot-out
4. Arsenal, Charlton Athletic, Chelsea, Crystal Palace, Millwall, Queens Park Rangers, Tottenham Hotspur and Wimbledon
5. Gianni Infantino
6. San Marino
7. Ryan Giggs (in 2009)
8. The Dubious Goals Committee
9. Aston Villa
10. Sean Bean
11. The UEFA Cup Winners' Cup
12. The UEFA Intertoto Cup

EUROPEAN CULT HEROES

1. Hernán Crespo
2. Dino Baggio
3. Youri Djorkaeff
4. Rubén Sosa
5. Tomas Brolin
6. Attilio Lombardo
7. Stefan Effenberg
8. Bryan Roy
9. Faustino Asprilla
10. Iván Zamorano
11. Michael Laudrup
12. Hristo Stoichkov
13. Jean-Pierre Papin
14. Rui Costa
15. Jean Tigana

BLASTS FROM THE PAST

1. Andrei Kanchelskis
2. Juninho
3. Tony Yeboah
4. Jay-Jay Okocha
5. Tim Sherwood
6. Julian Dicks

STANDS

1. Crystal Palace
2. Fulham
3. Manchester City
4. Newcastle United
5. Southampton
6. Arsenal
7. Celtic
8. Aston Villa
9. Nottingham Forest
10. Preston North End
11. Rangers

CLOSEST GROUNDS

1. Dundee and Dundee United
2. Nottingham Forest and Notts County
3. Liverpool and Everton
4. Aston Villa and Birmingham City
5. Sheffield Wednesday and Sheffield United
6. Four
7. Five

BOXING (EASY)

(PAGE 71)

MUHAMMAD ALI

1. **B:** Cassius Clay
2. **B:** The Greatest
3. **C:** Vietnam War
4. **A:** Heavyweight
5. **B:** 'Sting like a bee'
6. **B:** *Parkinson*
7. **A:** Will Smith

ANTHONY JOSHUA

1. **C:** London 2012
2. **A:** Wladimir Klitschko
3. **B:** AJ
4. **A:** 1
5. **C:** Tyson Fury
6. **B:** An OBE
7. **A:** London

TRIVIA

1. **A:** A Ring
2. **A:** The Marquess of Queensbury
3. **A:** Hook
4. **B:** The belt
5. **C:** Southpaw
6. **B:** Throw in the Towel
7. **C:** Superweight
8. **C:** Undisputed Champion
9. **C:** 12
10. **B:** Jungle; **A:** Manila

BOXING (MEDIUM)

(PAGE 74)

WHAT'S IN A NAME?

1. Wladimir Klitschko **Dr Steelhammer**
2. Vitali Klitschko **Dr Ironfist**
3. Evander Holyfield **The Real Deal**
4. Mike Tyson **Iron**
5. Joe Frazier **Smokin'**
6. Naseem Hamed **Prince**
7. Joe Louis **The Brown Bomber**
8. Floyd Mayweather **Money**
9. Tyson Fury **The Gypsy King**
10. Deontay Wilder **The Bronze Bomber**
11. Manny Pacquiao **PacMan**
12. Ricky Hatton **The Hit Man**
13. Nikolai Valuev **The Beast from the East**

EY, BIG FELLA

1. Nikolai Valuev (7 ft 0 in)
2. Tyson Fury (6 ft 9 in)
3. Lennox Lewis (6 ft 5 in)
4. Muhammad Ali (6 ft 3 in)
5. Mike Tyson (5 ft 10 in)
6. Floyd Mayweather Jr. (5 ft 8 in)
7. Manny Pacquiao (5 ft 5.5 in)

RECORD BREAKERS

1. Henry Cooper
2. Barry McGuigan
3. Nicola Adams
4. Frank Bruno
5. Bernard Hopkins
6. Joe Calzaghe
7. Conor McGregor

TRIVIA

1. Evander Holyfield
2. Don King
3. Red and blue
4. Wladimir Klitschko
5. 10
6. Rope-a-dope
7. Rabbit punch
8. Technical knockout
9. Mike Tyson
10. Cinderella Man
11. Rio 2016
12. World Boxing Association, World Boxing Council, World Boxing Organization and International Boxing Federation
13. Liam Neeson
14. Deontay Wilder

NAME THAT NATIONALITY

1. Vitali Klitschko **Ukrainian**
2. Nikolai Valuev **Russian**
3. Manny Pacquiao **Filipino**
4. Juan Manuel Márquez **Mexican**
5. Katie Taylor **Irish**

BOXING (HARD)

(PAGE 77)

SIX OF THE BEST UPSETS

1. Oliver McCall
2. Sugar Ray Leonard
3. Andy Ruiz Jr.
4. Buster Douglas
5. Cassius Clay
6. Leon Spinks

TRASH TALKING

1. Muhammad Ali
2. Floyd Mayweather Jr.
3. Mike Tyson
4. Lennox Lewis
5. David Haye
6. Chris Eubank
7. Tyson Fury

TRIVIA

1. Rocky Marciano
2. 1996 (Atlanta)
3. Sir Henry Cooper
4. Jack Johnson
5. Manny Pacquiao
6. Bernard Hopkins
7. Muhammad Ali
8. Little toe
9. Marvin Hagler
10. MGM Grand
11. Herbie Hide
12. Riddick Bowe
13. WBA (founded in 1962)
14. Jermain Taylor (Middleweight, 2005); Bernard Hopkins (Middleweight, 2001–2005); Terence Crawford (Light Welterweight, 2015–2017); Oleksandr Usyk (Cruiserweight, 2018–2019); Josh Taylor (Light Welterweight, 2021–)

MATCH THE QUOTE WITH THE PERSON

1. 'Everybody has a plan until they get punched in the face.' **Mike Tyson**
2. 'I hated every minute of training, but I said, "Don't quit. Suffer now and live the rest of your life as a champion."' **Muhammad Ali**
3. 'Boxing is the toughest and loneliest sport in the world.' **Frank Bruno**
4. 'I remember as a little boy I ate one meal a day and sometimes slept in the street. I will never forget that, and it inspires me to fight hard, stay strong and remember all the people of my country, trying to achieve better for themselves.' **Manny Pacquiao**
5. 'Why waltz with a guy for 10 rounds when you can knock him out in one?' **Rocky Marciano**
6. 'Sure the fight was fixed. I fixed it with my right hand.' **George Foreman**
7. 'I think my greatest achievement in boxing is my following.' **Ricky Hatton**
8. 'I don't like to get hit, who likes it? I probably wouldn't do this sport if I was getting hit that much.' **Wladimir Klitschko**
9. 'Man, I hit him with punches that'd bring down the walls of a city.' **Joe Frazier**

WEIGHT DIVISIONS

1. Minimumweight
2. Flyweight
3. Bantamweight
4. Featherweight
5. Lightweight
6. Welterweight
7. Middleweight
8. Cruiserweight
9. Heavyweight

BOXING AND HOLLYWOOD

1. Wladimir Klitschko and Lennox Lewis
2. Joe Frazier
3. Sugar Ray Leonard
4. Denzel Washington
5. Jake LaMotta
6. Mike Tyson

WHERE IN THE WORLD?

1. Saudi Arabia
2. Democratic Republic of Congo (formerly Zaire)
3. New York (Madison Square Garden)
4. Gibraltar
5. David Haye
6. The Philippines

FIRST-ROUND KOs

1. Michael Spinks
2. Muhammad Ali
3. Chris Eubank
4. 'Prince' Naseem Hamed
5. Nigel Benn
6. Sonny Liston

SPLIT DRAWS

1. Manny Pacquiao and Juan Manuel Márquez
2. Evander Holyfield and Lennox Lewis
3. Sugar Ray Leonard and Tommy Hearns
4. Tyson Fury and Deontay Wilder
5. Nigel Benn and Chris Eubank

GOING FOR GOLD

1. Lennox Lewis (super heavyweight) **Seoul 1988**
2. George Foreman (heavyweight) **Mexico City 1968**
3. James DeGale (middleweight) **Beijing 2008**
4. Anthony Joshua (super heavyweight) **London 2012**
5. Wladimir Klitschko (super heavyweight) **Atlanta 1996**
6. Audley Harrison (super heavyweight) **Sydney 2000**
7. Joe Frazier (heavyweight) **Tokyo 1964**
8. Oscar de la Hoya (lightweight) **Barcelona 1992**
9. Floyd Patterson (middleweight) **Helsinki 1952**
10. Cassius Clay (light heavyweight) **Rome 1960**

CRICKET (EASY)

(PAGE 85)

TRIVIA

1. **B:** 11
2. **A:** The Ashes
3. **B:** Lord's
4. **C:** England
5. **B:** Two
6. **C:** Six
7. **B:** Umpire
8. **C:** Australia
9. **A:** Ben Stokes
10. **A:** 40
11. **B:** 100
12. **A:** West Indies
13. **B:** Phil Tufnell

CRICKETING TERMS AND ABBREVIATIONS

1. **C:** Australia
2. **A:** Around the batsman's feet
3. **B:** Maiden
4. **A:** The corridor of uncertainty
5. **A:** Tail enders
6. **A:** Leg before wicket
7. **B:** No ball
8. **B:** Howzat!
9. **A:** Around the head or upper body
10. **C:** A Full toss
11. **B:** Seam

EQUIPMENT

1. **C:** Three
2. **C:** Bails
3. **A:** Box
4. **C:** Willow
5. **A:** White
6. **B:** Leather

FIELD OF PLAY

1. **C:** Stupid long leg
2. **A:** Third man
3. **A:** Wicket-keeper
4. **B:** 22 yards
5. **A:** Cow corner
6. **A:** Rope
7. **A:** Six
8. **B:** Four

NICKNAMES

1. **C:** South Africa
2. **A:** Andrew Flintoff
3. **B:** Ian Botham
4. **B:** Barmy Army
5. **A:** Fanatics
6. **C:** New Zealand

STRICTLY CRICKET

1. **C:** Darren Gough
2. **B:** Mark Ramprakash
3. **C:** Phil Tufnell
4. **A:** Michael Vaughan
5. **B:** Graeme Swann

TRUE OR FALSE

1. True
2. False
3. True
4. False
5. True
6. False
7. True
8. True
9. False
10. False

CRICKET (MEDIUM)

(PAGE 91)

THE T20 BLAST

1. Derbyshire **Falcons**
2. Lancashire **Lightning**
3. Leicestershire **Foxes**
4. Northants **Steelbacks**
5. Notts **Outlaws**
6. Birmingham **Bears**
7. Worcestershire **Rapids**
8. Yorkshire **Vikings**
9. Essex **Eagles**
10. Kent **Spitfires**
11. Sussex **Sharks**

INDIAN PREMIER LEAGUE TEAMS

1. Chennai **Super Kings**
2. Delhi **Capitals**
3. Kolkata **Knight Riders**
4. Mumbai **Indians**
5. Punjab **Kings**
6. Rajasthan **Royals**
7. Bangalore **Royal Challengers**
8. Hyderabad **Sunrisers**

ANSWERS: CRICKET (MEDIUM)

LINE-UPS

England

1. Marcus Trescothick
2. Andrew Strauss
3. Michael Vaughan (c)
4. Ian Bell
5. Kevin Pietersen
6. Andrew Flintoff
7. Geraint Jones†
8. Ashley Giles
9. Matthew Hoggard
10. Steve Harmison
11. Simon Jones

Australia

1. Justin Langer
2. Matthew Hayden
3. Ricky Ponting (c)
4. Damien Martyn
5. Michael Clarke
6. Simon Katich
7. Adam Gilchrist†
8. Shane Warne
9. Brett Lee
10. Jason Gillespie
11. Michael Kasprowicz

ANAGRAMS

1. SONAR JOY **JASON ROY**
2. JINNY ROWBOATS **JONNY BAIRSTOW**
3. REO TOJO **JOE ROOT**
4. ANNIE GROOM **EOIN MORGAN**
5. BEES TONKS **BEN STOKES**
6. BRUTE JOLTS **JOS BUTTLER**
7. SOCK WASHIER **CHRIS WOAKES**
8. MULTIPLE TANK **LIAM PLUNKETT**
9. FORCE JARAH **JOFRA ARCHER**
10. RADIAL DISH **ADIL RASHID**
11. WORD AMOK **MARK WOOD**

LESSER-KNOWN CRICKET-PLAYING NATIONS

1. Kenya
2. Netherlands
3. Canada
4. Scotland
5. United Arab Emirates
6. Namibia
7. Bermuda

WHAT HAPPENED NEXT?

1. Harmison bowls a ball so wide that Andrew Flintoff collects it at second slip.
2. Brathwaite smashes four consecutive sixes to win with two balls to spare.
3. The ball comes in, deflects off Stokes's outstretched bat and races to the boundary earning England six runs.
4. Bancroft rubs the ball with a strip of sandpaper and is caught doing so by television coverage, in what became known as the 'Sandpapergate' scandal.
5. Umpire Ross Emerson no-balls Murali for throwing, leading to a 12-minute stand-off before the game eventually resumes.
6. Chappell rolls an underarm delivery towards Brian McKechnie who blocks it before throwing his bat in the air in disgust while the crowd boos.
7. Warne bowls a ball that lands several inches outside the line of Gatting's leg stump before it spins dramatically and clips the off stump, leaving Gatting staring at the pitch for several seconds.

SLEDGING

1. Andrew Flintoff
2. Darren Gough
3. Shane Warne
4. Merv Hughes
5. Dennis Lillee
6. Viv Richards

TROPHIES

1. Warne–Muralitharan Trophy **Australia–Sri Lanka**
2. Wisden Trophy **England–West Indies**
3. Freedom Trophy **India–South Africa**
4. Border–Gavaskar Trophy **Australia–India**
5. Sir Vivian Richards Trophy **South Africa–West Indies**
6. Frank Worrell Trophy **Australia–West Indies**
7. Trans–Tasman Trophy **Australia–New Zealand**
8. Basil D'Oliveira Trophy **England–South Africa**
9. Pataudi Trophy **England–India**
10. Sobers–Tissera Trophy **West Indies–Sri Lanka**

RECORD-BREAKING BATSMEN

Name	Runs	Country	Test Career Span
Sachin Tendulkar	15,921	India	1989–2013
Ricky Ponting	13,378	Australia	1995–2012
Jacques Kallis	13,289	South Africa	1995–2013
Rahul Dravid	13,288	India	1996–2012
Alastair Cook	12,472	England	2006–2018
Kumar Sangakkara	12,400	Sri Lanka	2000–2015
Brian Lara	11,953	West Indies	1990–2006
Shivnarine Chanderpaul	11,867	West Indies	1994–2015
Mahela Jayawardene	11,814	Sri Lanka	1997–2014
Allan Border	11,174	Australia	1978–1994
Steve Waugh	10,927	Australia	1985–2004
Sunil Gavaskar	10,122	India	1971–1987
Younis Khan	10,099	Pakistan	2000–2017

RECORD-BREAKING BOWLERS

Name	Country	Wickets
Muttiah Muralitharan	Sri Lanka	800
Shane Warne	Australia	708
James Anderson*	England	630
Anil Kumble	India	619
Glenn McGrath	Australia	563
Stuart Broad*	England	524
Courtney Walsh	West Indies	519
Dale Steyn*	South Africa	439
Kapil Dev	India	434
Rangana Herath	Sri Lanka	433
Richard Hadlee	New Zealand	431
Shaun Pollock	South Africa	421
Harbhajan Singh	India	417
Wasim Akram	Pakistan	414
Ravichandran Ashwin*	India	413
Curtly Ambrose	West Indies	405

TOP TEST SCORES

1.	400*	The Prince	**Brian Lara**
2.	380	Australian left-handed batsman who opened with Justin Langer	**Matthew Hayden**
3.	375	The Prince again!	**Brian Lara**
4.	374	Sri Lankan legend who retired from Test cricket in 2014	**Mahela Jayawardene**
5.	365*	One of the best all-rounders to play the game, he was made one of ten National Heroes of Barbados by act of Parliament in 1998	**Garfield Sobers**
6.	364	Yorkshire legend, former England captain and later Test selector and broadcaster	**Len Hutton**
7.	340	Sri Lankan all-rounder who hit a James Anderson over for six fours in his final Test innings in 2007	**Sanath Jayasuriya**
8.	337	First Pakistani to score a triple hundred, which he did in 1958; also reached a record-breaking 499 for Karachi in 1959	**Hanif Mohammad**
9.	336*	England captain before and after the Second World War	**Wally Hammond**
10.	335*	Australian vice-captain from 2015 to 2018 but suspended from cricket for a year after the ball tampering scandal of 2018	**David Warner**
11=	334	Legend who finished his career with a scarcely believable average of 99.94	**Don Bradman**
11=	334*	Australian opening batsman and captain from 1994 to 1999	**Mark Taylor**
13=	333	Essex legend, England opening batsman and captain from 1988 to 1993	**Graham Gooch**
13=	333	West Indian big-hitter with the most sixes in international cricket, as at August 2021	**Chris Gayle**

KNIGHTS OF THE REALM

1. **Don Bradman** (Australia, knighted 1949)
2. **Richard Hadlee** (New Zealand, knighted 1990)
3. **Viv Richards** (West Indies, knighted 1999)
4. **Ian Botham** (England, knighted 2007)
5. **Richie Richardson** (West Indies, 2014)
6. **Curtly Ambrose** (West Indies, 2014)
7. **Alastair Cook** (England, 2019)
8. **Geoffrey Boycott** (England, 2019)
9. **Andrew Strauss** (England, 2019)
10. **Gordon Greenidge** (West Indies, 2020)
11. **Clive Lloyd** (West Indies, 2020)

COUNTY LEGENDS

1. Yorkshire
2. Lancashire
3. Essex
4. Surrey
5. Middlesex
6. Durham
7. Worcestershire
8. W.G. Grace
9. Ian Botham

MATCH THE ENDS TO THE STADIUMS

1. Nursery End, Pavilion End **Lord's**
2. Birmingham End (previously City End), Pavilion **Edgbaston**
3. James Anderson End, Brian Statham End **Old Trafford**
4. Radcliffe Road End, Pavilion End **Trent Bridge**
5. River End, Marcus Trescothick Pavilion End **County Ground, Taunton**
6. Lumley End, Finchale End **Riverside Ground (Chester-le-Street)**
7. Vauxhall End, Pavilion End **The Oval**

8. River Taff End, Cathedral Road End **Sophia Gardens**
9. Ashley Down Road End, Bristol Pavilion End **Bristol County Ground (Nevil Road)**
10. Kirkstall Lane End, Football Stand End **Headingley**

WHO ARE THEY ON ABOUT?

1. James Anderson
2. Brett Lee
3. Allan Donald
4. Wasim Akram

TRIVIA

1. Marylebone Cricket Club
2. Imran Khan
3. William Gilbert
4. Don Bradman
5. Kangaroo and Emu
6. England
7. Warwickshire
8. Phil Neville
9. Ian Botham
10. Lord's
11. Wales
12. Andrew Flintoff
13. Specsavers
14. Australia
15. Hansie Cronje

CRICKET (HARD)

(PAGE 102)

HEAD AND SHOULDERS ABOVE THE REST

1.	7 ft 1 in	Pakistani left-arm fast bowler 2010–19	**Mohammad Irfan**
2.	6 ft 8 in	West Indian right-arm fast bowler 1977–87	**Joel Garner**
3.	6 ft 8 in	Australian left-arm fast-medium bowler 1985–92	**Bruce Reid**
4.	6 ft 7 in	English right-arm fast-medium bowler 2005–13	**Chris Tremlett**
5.	6 ft 7 in	West Indian right-arm fast bowler 1998–2000	**Curtly Ambrose**
6.	6 ft 7 in	West Indian all-rounder 2013–	**Jason Holder**
7.	6 ft 7 in	English right-arm fast bowler 2010–17	**Steven Finn**
8.	6 ft 6 in	New Zealand right-arm fast-medium bowler 2001–12	**Jacob Oram**
9.	6 ft 6 in	English all-rounder 1972–77	**Tony Grieg**
10.	6 ft 6 in	Australian left-arm fast bowler 2010–	**Mitchell Starc**
11.	6 ft 6 in	Pakistani left-arm fast bowler 2018–	**Shaheen Afridi**
12.	6 ft 6 in	Australian fast-medium bowler 1993–2007	**Glenn McGrath**
13.	6 ft 5 in	South African right-arm fast bowler 2006–18	**Morné Morkel**

METHODS OF DISMISSAL

1. Bowled
2. Caught
3. Leg Before Wicket
4. Run Out
5. Stumped
6. Hit The Ball Twice
7. Hit Wicket
8. Obstructing The Field (also incorporates the former method of dismissal *Handled the Ball* as of 2017)
9. Timed Out
10. Retired Out

FIELDING POSITIONS

1. Wicket-keeper
2. Slips
3. Gully
4. Leg Slip
5. Leg Gully
6. Silly Point
7. Silly Mid-off
8. Short Leg
9. Silly Mid-on
10. Point
11. Backward Point
12. Mid-off
13. Cover
14. Extra Cover
15. Mid-on
16. Square Leg
17. Backward Square Leg
18. Mid-wicket
19. Short Fine Leg
20. Fly Slip
21. Third Man
22. Deep Point
23. Deep Backward Point
24. Deep Cover
25. Deep Extra Cover
26. Long Off
27. Deep Fine Leg
28. Long Leg
29. Deep Square Leg
30. Deep Mid-wicket
31. Cow Corner
32. Long On

WHERE IN THE WORLD?

1. Queen's Park Oval, Trinidad
2. Newlands, Cape Town
3. Wanderers Stadium (the Bullring), Johannesburg
4. National Stadium, Karachi
5. Wankhede Stadium, Mumbai
6. Gaddafi Stadium, Lahore
7. Galle International
8. Eden Gardens, Kolkata
9. WACA, Perth
10. MCG, Melbourne
11. SCG, Sydney
12. Eden Park, Auckland
13. Basin Reserve, Wellington

NICKNAMES

1. Punter – **Ricky Ponting** (named by Shane Warne for his tendency to have a punt on the dog races back in the 1990s)
2. The Little Master – **Sachin Tendulkar** (due to small stature and general brilliance)
3. Mr 360 – **AB de Villiers** (named for his ability to hit the ball anywhere)
4. Beefy – **Ian Botham** (for his full figure)
5. Freddie – **Andrew Flintoff** (Freddie Flintstone)
6. The Pigeon – **Glenn McGrath** (nicknamed by New South Wales teammate Brad McNamara after seeing Glenn's skinny legs)
7. Chef – **Alastair Cook** (in reference to his culinary surname)
8. The Rawalpindi Express – **Shoaib Akhtar** (in reference to where he was born and the fact he steamed in to bowl like a train)
9. The Cat – **Phil Tufnell** (named for his love of a catnap, especially in the dressing room)
10. The Wall – **Rahul Dravid** (in reference to facing the highest number of balls in Test cricket and his solid defence. Dravid himself said modestly: 'I think, it probably came out after one of my long, typically, maybe boring innings')

11. The King of Spain – **Ashley Giles** (Genius mistake involving his club Warwickshire ordering mugs with 'King of Spin' printed on them in 2001 only to suffer a catastrophic typo)
12. Mr Cricket – **Mike Hussey** (apparently given to him by Andrew Flintoff after he looked like he was really enjoying himself out in the middle on a terrible day)

ANAGRAMS

England Test captains:

1. ALMANAC HIVE HUG **MICHAEL VAUGHAN**
2. AMINO BATH **IAN BOTHAM**
3. DOWN NAFF TRIFLE **ANDREW FLINTOFF**
4. OVERDID WAG **DAVID GOWER**
5. EERILY EMBARK **MIKE BREARLEY**
6. EASTWARDS RUNS **ANDREW STRAUSS**
7. SAUNAS SHINERS **NASSER HUSSAIN**
8. HARMONIC ATHLETE **MICHAEL ATHERTON**
9. ACHROMA GOGH **GRAHAM GOOCH**
10. OREO JOT **JOE ROOT**
11. RASCAL TWEET **ALEC STEWART**
12. GAME KITTING **MIKE GATTING**
13. BOWL IBLIS **BOB WILLIS**
14. COFFEE GROTTY YOB **GEOFFREY BOYCOTT**
15. CREW GAG **W.G. GRACE**

Leading run scorers in Tests:

1. AUCKLAND HINTERS **SACHIN TENDULKAR**
2. CRYPT OINKING **RICKY PONTING**
3. JACKIE SQUALLS **JACQUES KALLIS**
4. CROATIA KOLAS **ALASTAIR COOK**
5. DAD HURL RIVA **RAHUL DRAVID**
6. ARGUS KANAKA MARK **KUMAR SANGAKKARA**

7. BAR LARINA **BRIAN LARA**
8. ANNUAL CHIP REVARNISHED **SHIVNARINE CHANDERPAUL**
9. DEJA RENEWAL YAMAHA **MAHELA JAYAWARDENE**
10. ANDORRA BELL **ALLAN BORDER**

BUNNIES

1. Graham Gooch **Malcolm Marshall** (16 dismissals)
2. Michael Atherton **Glenn McGrath** (19 dismissals)
3. Ian Healy **Courtney Walsh** (15 dismissals)
4. Nasser Hussain **Shane Warne** (11 dismissals)
5. Mark Waugh **Curtly Ambrose** (15 dismissals)
6. Greg Chappell **Derek Underwood** (13 dismissals)
7. Allan Border **Ian Botham** (12 dismissals)
8. Mark Boucher **Muttiah Muralitharan** (12 dismissals)
9. David Warner **Stuart Broad** (12 dismissals)
10. Ben Stokes **Ravichandran Ashwin** (11 dismissals)
11. Sunil Gavaskar **Derek Underwood** (12 dismissals)
12. Ricky Ponting **Harbhajan Singh** (10 dismissals)

CRICKET-PLAYING COUNTIES

Here are the names of the counties in Division One and Division Two:

1. Durham
2. Yorkshire
3. Lancashire
4. Derbyshire
5. Nottinghamshire
6. Leicestershire
7. Warwickshire
8. Northamptonshire
9. Worcestershire
10. Gloucestershire
11. Essex
12. Glamorgan
13. Middlesex
14. Somerset
15. Hampshire
16. Surrey
17. Kent
18. Sussex

ALL TIME WORLD CUP XI

1. Sachin Tendulkar
2. Rohit Sharma
3. Ricky Ponting (c)
4. Kumar Sangakkara (wk)
5. Viv Richards
6. AB de Villiers
7. Lance Klusener
8. Wasim Akram
9. Mitchell Starc
10. Glenn McGrath
11. Muttiah Muralitharan

TRIVIA

1. Barbados
2. David Shepherd
3. James Laker (10/53 for England v Australia in 1956) and Anil Kumble (10/74 for India v Pakistan in 1999)
4. Kumar Sangakkara
5. Sri Lanka
6. Monty Panesar (4.89 average)
7. Phil Tufnell (5.1 average)
8. Graham Gooch
9. Mankading (after Vinoo Mankad)
10. A lime tree known as the St Lawrence Lime
11. Five
12. Six overs
13. 'Fake fielding' by pretending to throw the ball towards the stumps when the ball had actually passed him. Penalty runs were awarded to the opposing team for violating Law 41.5.
14. The ball went through the space between the middle and off stumps but did not dislodge the bails
15. Chris Morris (bought by Rajasthan Royals for approximately £1.57 million)

MASTER BLASTERS

1. Matthew Hayden, who had scored 380 against Zimbabwe in October 2003
2. Graham Gooch, who scored 333 and 123 (a combined 456) against India in 1990
3. Kyle Mayers
4. Rohit Sharma
5. Jason Roy
6. Aaron Finch
7. AB de Villiers
8. Yuvraj Singh
9. Javed Miandad
10. Sir Garfield Sobers

DARTS (EASY)

(PAGE 115)

TRIVIA

1. **A:** Circle
2. **B:** 501
3. **C:** 180
4. **B:** 3
5. **A:** Bullseye
6. **B:** 40
7. **C:** The Oche
8. **B:** Three
9. **C:** Eric Bristow
10. **A:** Phil 'The Power' Taylor

DARTS (MEDIUM)

(PAGE 117)

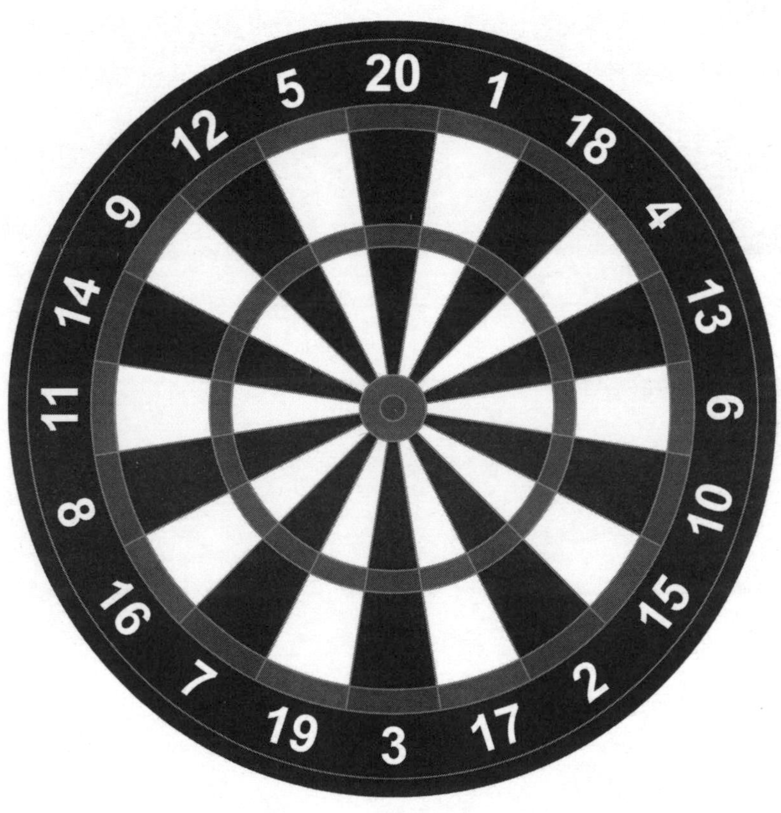

NICKNAMES

1. Wolfie **Martin Adams**
2. The Power **Phil Taylor**
3. The Count **Ted Hankey**
4. The Crafty Cockney **Eric Bristow**
5. Jackpot **Adrian Lewis**
6. The Flying Scotsman **Gary Anderson**
7. Voltage **Rob Cross**
8. The Matchstick **Co Stompé**
9. Old Stoneface **John Lowe**
10. Snakebite **Peter Wright**
11. Darth Maple **John Part**

TRIVIA

1. Lakeside Country Club
2. Indigo at the O2 in London
3. Alexandra Palace
4. Dennis Priestley
5. Tungsten
6. 451mm (to within 50mm, anything between 401mm to 501mm is alright!)
7. Eric Bristow

DARTS (HARD)

(PAGE 119)

TRIVIA

1. Sid Waddell
2. Raymond van Barneveld, in 2009
3. Trina Gulliver
4. Fallon Sherrock
5. 1992
6. John Part in 2003; Raymond van Barneveld in 2007; Michael van Gerwen in 2014, 2017 and 2019
7. 2001
8. 2010
9. The Winter Gardens in Blackpool
10. Barry Hearn

WALK-ON MUSIC

1. 'Eye of the Tiger' by Survivor **Raymond van Barneveld**
2. 'Seven Nation Army' by the White Stripes **Michael van Gerwen**
3. 'Can't Touch This' by MC Hammer **Andy Hamilton**
4. 'The Imperial March' by John Williams **John Part**
5. 'Cotton Eye Joe' by Rednex **John Walton**
6. 'The Power' by Snap **Phil Taylor**
7. 'Don't Stop the Party' by Pitbull **Peter Wright**
8. 'Hungry Like the Wolf' by Duran Duran **Martin Adams**
9. 'Jump Around' by House of Pain **Gary Anderson**

ANSWERS: DARTS (HARD)

ANAGRAMS

1. CORR SOBS **ROB CROSS**
2. JAN THORP **JOHN PART**
3. JAW SEAMED **JAMES WADE**
4. APRIL HOTLY **PHIL TAYLOR**
5. BOGEY GOBBER **BOBBY GEORGE**
6. CLOWN JOYSKI **JOCKY WILSON**
7. SORBIC WRITE **ERIC BRISTOW**
8. GIRTH PEWTER **PETER WRIGHT**
9. CREWING PREY **GERWYN PRICE**
10. PINKIE TAVERN **KEVIN PAINTER**
11. GRUNT LANDER **GLEN DURRANT**
12. SALARIED WIN **ADRIAN LEWIS**
13. DRAGONS YEARN **GARY ANDERSON**
14. ABNORMAL DANNY REVVED **RAYMOND VAN BARNEVELD**
15. CHINA ENGRAVE MEWL **MICHAEL VAN GERWEN**

F1 (EASY)

(PAGE 125)

TRIVIA

1. **B:** Chequered black and white
2. **A:** Safety car
3. **C:** Grand Prix
4. **A:** Pole
5. **B:** The pits
6. **C:** Red
7. **B:** Tyres
8. **A:** Germany
9. **B:** Brazil
10. **B:** 1950s
11. **B:** Chicane
12. **A:** Stewards
13. **A:** New Zealand
14. **B:** Scotland
15. **B:** Italy
16. **A:** Button
17. **B:** 2007
18. **C:** Nico Rosberg
19. **A:** Toyota
20. **B:** Murray Walker
21. **B:** Ferrari
22. **C:** Bernie Ecclestone
23. **B:** Silverstone
24. **A:** 5
25. **B:** 1

F1 (MEDIUM)

(PAGE 128)

BLACK FLAGS

1. Juan Pablo Montoya
2. Ayrton Senna
3. Michael Schumacher
4. Alain Prost
5. Nigel Mansell

1980s

1. Alan Jones
2. Brands Hatch
3. Nelson Piquet
4. Niki Lauda and Alain Prost
5. Ayrton Senna
6. Nigel Mansell
7. Ayrton Senna and Alain Prost
8. Gerhard Berger

POINTS

1. 1st 25
2. 2nd 18
3. 3rd 15

NAME THOSE CHAMPIONS

1. Juan Manuel Fangio
2. Nigel Mansell
3. Fernando Alonso
4. Ayrton Senna
5. Graham and Damon Hill and Keke and Nico Rosberg
6. Jacques Villeneuve
7. Jenson Button
8. James Hunt
9. Alain Prost
10. Michael Schumacher and Sebastian Vettel

TRIVIA

1. Graham Hill
2. Monaco Grand Prix; Indianapolis 500; 24 Hours of Le Mans
3. Stirling Moss
4. Eddie Irvine
5. Monaco
6. Charles Leclerc
7. Max Verstappen
8. Six
9. Nigel Mansell
10. Slicks
11. Ayrton Senna

F1 (HARD)

(PAGE 132)

HOST COUNTRIES

1. Argentina
2. Australia
3. Austria
4. Azerbaijan
5. Bahrain
6. Belgium
7. Brazil
8. Canada
9. China
10. France
11. Germany
12. Hungary
13. India
14. Italy
15. Japan
16. Malaysia
17. Mexico
18. Monaco
19. Morocco
20. Netherlands
21. Portugal
22. Russia
23. San Marino
24. Saudi Arabia
25. Singapore
26. South Africa
27. South Korea
28. Spain
29. Sweden
30. Switzerland
31. Turkey
32. United Arab Emirates
33. United Kingdom
34. United States

TEAMMATES

1. Fernando Alonso (2007), Heikki Kovalainen (2008–9), Jenson Button (2010–12), Nico Rosberg (2013–16), Valtteri Bottas (2017–present)
2. Mark Webber (2009–13), Daniel Ricciardo (2014), Kimi Räikkönen (2015–18), Charles Leclerc (2019–20), Lance Stroll (2021–)

TRIVIA

1. Nick Heidfeld
2. 2014, while Sebastian Vettel defended his 2013 title
3. Stirling Moss
4. Damon Hill
5. Jack Brabham (1978); Stirling Moss (2000); Jackie Stewart (2001); Lewis Hamilton (2020)
6. Monza (70); Monaco (66); Silverstone (55); Spa-Francorchamps (53)
7. 1986
8. Nigel Mansell
9. Northamptonshire
10. Lewis Hamilton
11. 5
12. Sparkling wine
13. Rubens Barrichello and David Coulthard
14. Alberto Ascari
15. Peter Gethin
16. Emerson Fittipaldi
17. Jack Brabham
18. Michael Schumacher
19. 15,000
20. Johnny Herbert
21. Alfa Romeo
22. Rubens Barrichello
23. Martin Brundle
24. Alfa Romeo, Ferrari, Mercedes-Benz and Maserati
25. Sergio Pérez

GOLF (EASY)

(PAGE 137)

TRIVIA

1. **B:** 18
2. **A:** Woods, irons and a putter
3. **A:** Sand wedge
4. **B:** Caddie
5. **C:** Fore!
6. **A:** Links
7. **C:** Green
8. **B:** Scotland
9. **C:** Out of bounds
10. **B:** Par
11. **C:** Eagle
12. **A:** The honour
13. **B:** Tee
14. **B:** Driving range
15. **C:** Donald Trump
16. **B:** Divot
17. **C:** George W. Bush
18. **A:** *Happy Gilmore*
19. **B:** *Caddyshack*
20. **C:** Green jacket

GOLF (MEDIUM)

(PAGE 140)

NICKNAMES

1. El Niño **Sergio García**
2. Golden Bear **Jack Nicklaus**
3. Great White Shark **Greg Norman**
4. Lefty **Phil Mickelson**
5. Walrus **Craig Stadler**
6. Wild Thing **John Daly**
7. The Big Easy **Ernie Els**
8. Boom Boom **Fred Couples**
9. The King **Arnold Palmer**
10. The Postman **Ian Poulter**

NATIONAL FIRSTS

1. Germany **Bernhard Langer**
2. Wales **Ian Woosnam**
3. Canada **Mike Weir**
4. Fiji **Vijay Singh**
5. Rep. of Ireland **Pádraig Harrington**
6. Sweden **Henrik Stenson**
7. Italy **Francesco Molinari**
8. Japan **Hideki Matsuyama**

RYDER CUP CAPTAINS

Year	Europe	US
2020 (21)	**Pádraig Harrington**	**Steve Stricker**
2018	**Thomas Bjørn**	**Jim Furyk**
2016	**Darren Clarke**	**Davis Love III**
2014	**Paul McGinley**	**Tom Watson**
2012	**José María Olazábal**	**Davis Love III**
2010	**Colin Montgomerie**	**Corey Pavin**
2008	**Nick Faldo**	**Paul Azinger**
2006	**Ian Woosnam**	**Tom Lehman**
2004	**Bernhard Langer**	**Hal Sutton**
2002	**Sam Torrance**	**Curtis Strange**
1999	**Mark James**	**Ben Crenshaw**

MOST WEEKS AT NUMBER ONE

Weeks at No. 1	Clue	Name
683	Winner of 15 majors, the last of which (as at July 2021) was the 2019 Masters	**Tiger Woods**
331	Australian legend who won The Open in 1986 and 1993	**Greg Norman**
127	American who won the US Open in 2016 and the Masters in 2020	**Dustin Johnson**
106	Northern Irishman who won his first major in 2011	**Rory McIlroy**
97	Englishman who won the Masters back to back in 1989 and 1990	**Nick Faldo**

THE MAJORS

1. The Masters, PGA Championship, US Open, The Open
2. The Open (1860), US Open (1895), PGA Championship (1916), The Masters (1934)

GOLF (HARD)

(PAGE 143)

ONLY THREE

1. Jack Nicklaus, Tiger Woods, Rory McIlroy
2. Luke Donald, Lee Westwood, Jon Rahm (who became world number 1 in July 2020 and won the US Open in 2021)

OPEN VENUES

1. Old Course at St Andrews
2. Muirfield
3. Royal St George's
4. Royal Liverpool
5. Royal Troon
6. Royal Lytham & St Annes
7. Carnoustie
8. Royal Portrush
9. Royal Birkdale
10. Turnberry

ANAGRAMS

Golfers:

1. KIMCHI POLLENS **PHIL MICKELSON**
2. GOOD WRITES **TIGER WOODS**
3. CAIRO SAGGIER **SERGIO GARCIA**
4. DIJON NOSHNUTS **DUSTIN JOHNSON**
5. COYLY MIRROR **RORY MCILROY**
6. TOWELED WOES **LEE WESTWOOD**
7. HARPED JOINTS **JORDAN SPIETH**
8. ABBA BOWNUTS **BUBBA WATSON**
9. JOINT USERS **JUSTIN ROSE**
10. MINTY EARMARK **MARTIN KAYMER**

ANSWERS: GOLF (HARD)

Golf courses:

ANATOLIAN AUGUST **AUGUSTA NATIONAL**
BABBLE CHEEP **PEBBLE BEACH**
SAGS WARS **SAWGRASS**
EMIR FLUID **MUIRFIELD**
BURR ENTRY **TURNBERRY**
RECUSATION **CARNOUSTIE**
ORTON **TROON**
HEN MAID **MEDINAH**
ARMED LARVA **VALDERRAMA**
STRAINS TWILIGHTS **WHISTLING STRAITS**

GOLF AROUND THE WORLD

1. USA (16,752)
2. Japan (3,169)
3. Canada (2,633)
4. England (2,270)
5. Australia (1,616)
6. Germany (1,050)
7. France (804)
8. South Korea (798)
9. Sweden (662)
10. Scotland (614)

CAREER GRAND SLAM

1. Ben Hogan
2. Gary Player
3. Jack Nicklaus
4. Tiger Woods

TRIVIA

1. 1979
2. Arnold Palmer
3. In 2015, they were among the first female members of the Royal and Ancient Golf Club of St Andrews
4. Troon (in 1978, upon the centenary of its founding)
5. USA and Great Britain & Ireland
6. Justin Rose
7. Darren Clarke
8. Nick Faldo
9. The 11th, 12th and 13th
10. Phil Mickelson (12)
11. Sergio García
12. Constantino Rocca
13. Martin Kaymer
14. Sandy Lyle
15. 15

WOMEN'S GOLF

1. ANA Inspiration, US Women's Open, Women's PGA Championship, Evian Championship, Women's British Open
2. Patty Berg
3. Annika Sörenstam
4. Michelle Wie
5. Laura Davies
6. Inbee Park

HORSE RACING (EASY)

(PAGE 149)

TRIVIA

1. **B:** Furlong
2. **C:** Going
3. **C:** Blinkers
4. **A:** Paddock
5. **B:** April
6. **C:** Aintree
7. **A:** Ascot
8. **C:** 56,000
9. **A:** Filly
10. **A:** USA
11. **C:** Red Rum
12. **A:** Seabiscuit
13. **B:** Frankie Dettori
14. **B:** The Derby

HORSE RACING (MEDIUM)

(PAGE 151)

GRAND NATIONAL

1. Rachael Blackmore
2. 1993
3. Becher's Brook
4. The Chair
5. Red Rum (1973, 1974 and 1977)
6. Liverpool
7. Jenny Pitman

ANAGRAMS

1. COAST **ASCOT**
2. REXTEE **EXETER**
3. RUBY WEN **NEWBURY**
4. ETCHERS **CHESTER**
5. RETINAE **AINTREE**
6. ANTHEM LECH **CHELTENHAM**
7. NOTED CARS **DONCASTER**
8. KNEW TAMER **NEWMARKET**
9. ELECT SWAN **NEWCASTLE**
10. DODO GO OW **GOODWOOD**
11. OUTER TEXT **UTTOXETER**
12. ALFRED KIPLING **LINGFIELD PARK**
13. DEMON SWOPS **EPSOM DOWNS**
14. CHOP DARK YAK **HAYDOCK PARK**
15. KART MONK PEP **KEMPTOWN PARK**
16. ONWARD SPANK **SANDOWN PARK**

ANSWERS: HORSE RACING (MEDIUM)

TRIVIA

1. The Queen
2. Peter O'Sullevan
3. AP McCoy
4. John McCririck
5. Channel 4
6. talkSPORT
7. Ascot
8. Cheltenham

FAMOUS OWNERS

1. Sir Alex Ferguson
2. Elizabeth Hurley
3. Ronnie Wood
4. Wayne Rooney
5. Michael Owen

HORSE RACING (HARD)

(PAGE 153)

ANAGRAMS

1. TIPSTER TOGGLE **LESTER PIGGOTT**
2. KART RENOTIFIED **FRANKIE DETTORI**
3. CAM COPY **AP MCCOY**
4. OLEFIN RANKLE **KIEREN FALLON**
5. BRUSHY LAW **RUBY WALSH**
6. CHEF JAN MORON **JOHN FRANCOME**
7. LOCALISER WIN **WILLIE CARSON**
8. DATED PREY **PAT EDDERY**
9. CORRODING SHARD **GORDON RICHARDS**
10. ACUTE SEVENTH **STEVE CAUTHEN**

GRAND NATIONAL

1. They each had odds of 100/1 to win the race
2. Two (in 1928)
3. Devon Loch
4. Richard Johnson
5. Second

NAME THAT HORSE

1. Shergar (Cher-ga)
2. Whistlejacket
3. Desert Orchid
4. Best Mate
5. L'Escargot
6. Miinnehoma
7. Earth Summit
8. Golden Miller

TRIVIA

1. York
2. Queen Anne
3. Sandringham
4. Yeats (winner from 2006–2009)
5. Queen Alexandra Stakes (2 miles, 5 furlongs and 143 yards [4,355 metres])
6. Shergar
7. Gordon Richards (1953) and AP McCoy (2016)
8. Best Mate
9. Tatersalls
10. Clare Balding
11. 2,000 Guineas Stakes, 1,000 Guineas Stakes, Epsom Oaks, Epsom Derby, St Leger Stakes
12. Kentucky Derby, Preakness Stakes, Belmont Stakes

RUGBY LEAGUE (EASY)

(PAGE 159)

TRIVIA

1. **B:** 13
2. **C:** 6
3. **A:** 4
4. **B:** 2
5. **B:** Castleford Caterpillars
6. **C:** The Challenge Cup
7. **A:** Six
8. **C:** Super League
9. **A:** Yorkshire
10. **B:** 40
11. **C:** 1954
12. **B:** Kevin Sinfield
13. **C:** 2000
14. **A:** True

INTERNATIONAL TEAM NICKNAMES

1. Kangaroos **Australia**
2. Lions **England**
3. Wolfhounds **Ireland**
4. Cedars **Lebanon**
5. Bears **Russia**
6. Tomahawks **United States**
7. Wolverines **Canada**

RUGBY LEAGUE (MEDIUM)

(PAGE 161)

CLUB MIX-UP

1. Castleford Tigers
2. Catalans Dragons
3. Huddersfield Giants
4. Hull Kingston Rovers
5. Leeds Rhinos
6. Leigh Centurions
7. Salford Red Devils
8. Wigan Warriors
9. Wakefield Trinity
10. Warrington Wolves

CODE SWAPPERS

1. Sonny Bill Williams
2. Chris Ashton
3. Shontayne Hape
4. Andy Farrell
5. Lesley Vainikolo
6. Brad Thorn
7. Jason Robinson
8. Martin Offiah

TRIVIA

1. England
2. Australia (11 times); Great Britain (three times); New Zealand (once)
3. Wigan
4. M62
5. Leeds Rhinos

RUGBY LEAGUE (HARD)

(PAGE 163)

2017 Rugby League World Cup teams:

1. Australia
2. Ireland
3. Papua New Guinea
4. United States
5. England
6. Italy
7. Samoa
8. Wales
9. Fiji
10. Lebanon
11. Scotland
12. France
13. New Zealand
14. Tonga

CHALLENGE CUP SPONSORSHIP

1. Kellogg's Nutrigrain
2. Powergen
3. Leeds Met Carnegie (known as the Carnegie Challenge Cup)
4. Tetley's
5. Ladbrokes
6. Coral

TRIVIA

1. Toronto Wolfpack
2. Huddersfield
3. 1999
4. Andy Farrell (2004), Kevin Sinfield (2012) and Tommy Makinson (2018)
5. Prince Harry
6. London Broncos
7. Paris Saint-Germain
8. Old Trafford
9. KCOM Stadium
10. The man of the match in the Challenge Cup Final
11. Clare Balding
12. St Helens
13. Sydney Roosters

SUPER LEAGUE TOP SCORERS

Player	Points	Club(s)	Career Span
Kevin Sinfield	3,443	Leeds	1997–2015
Danny Brough	2,462	Hull FC, Huddersfield, Wakefield	2005–2006, 2008–2020
Paul Deacon	2,415	Oldham, Bradford, Wigan	1997–2011
Andy Farrell	2,372	Wigan	1996–2004
Pat Richards	2,280	Wigan, Catalans	2006–2013, 2016

RUGBY UNION (EASY)

(PAGE 167)

TERMS AND RULES

1. **A:** Five
2. **B:** Three
3. **B:** A Conversion
4. **A:** 15
5. **A:** Six Nations Championship
6. **B:** Oval
7. **C:** Rugby Sevens
8. **C:** Scrum
9. **A:** Fly-half
10. **B:** H
11. **A:** Hooker
12. **B:** 80 minutes
13. **A:** Touch
14. **B:** Sin bin

NICKNAMES

1. New Zealand **All Blacks**
2. Australia **Wallabies**
3. Japan **Brave Blossoms**
4. Argentina **Los Pumas**
5. South Africa **Springboks**

SHIRTS

1. England **White**
2. Scotland **Dark blue**
3. Australia **Yellow**
4. Japan **Red and white hoops**
5. New Zealand **Black**
6. Argentina **Light blue and white hoops**
7. Wales **Red**
8. Ireland **Green**

STADIUMS

1. Murrayfield **Scotland**
2. Twickenham **England**
3. Millennium Stadium **Wales**
4. Lansdowne Road (Aviva Stadium) **Ireland**
5. Stadio Olimpico **Italy**
6. Ellis Park **South Africa**

TRUE OR FALSE

1. False
2. False
3. True
4. False
5. True
6. True
7. False

TRIVIA

1. **C:** Haka
2. **B:** Scotland
3. **B:** New Zealand
4. **A:** Four years
5. **B:** William Webb Ellis
6. **A:** Nelson Mandela
7. **A:** Zara Phillips
8. **B:** The Lions
9. **C:** Jonny Wilkinson
10. **A:** Bill Beaumont

RUGBY UNION (MEDIUM)

(PAGE 172)

MOST CAPPED ENGLAND PLAYERS

1. Jason Leonard
2. Ben Youngs
3. Dylan Hartley
4. Dan Cole
5. Owen Farrell
6. Jonny Wilkinson
7. Courtney Lawes

SYLLABLE GAME

1. MAR–TIN–JOHN–SON **(MARTIN JOHNSON)**
2. DAN–CAR–TA **(DAN CARTER)**
3. RICH–CHI–MAC–CAW **(RICHIE MCCAW)**
4. WILL–GREEN–WOOD **(WILL GREENWOOD)**
5. JAR–EMMY–GUST–COT **(JEREMY GUSCOTT)**
6. BEAU–DEN–BAR–RHETT **(BEAUDEN BARRETT)**
7. FAF–DICK–CLERK **(FAF DE KLERK)**
8. NICK–EAST–TOR **(NICK EASTER)**
9. STEW–ART–HOGG **(STUART HOGG)**
10. JOSH–LOO–SEA **(JOSH LEWSEY)**

TROPHIES

1. Calcutta Cup **England and Scotland**
2. Auld Alliance Trophy **Scotland and France**
3. Giuseppe Garibaldi Trophy **Italy and France**
4. Centenary Quaich **Ireland and Scotland**
5. Doddie Weir Cup **Scotland and Wales**
6. Bledisloe Cup **New Zealand and Australia**
7. Mandela Challenge Plate **Australia and South Africa**

8. Freedom Cup **New Zealand and South Africa**
9. Cook Cup **Australia and England**
10. Puma Trophy **Australia and Argentina**
11. Trophée des Bicentenaires **Australia and France**
12. Landsdowne Cup **Australia and Ireland**
13. Hopetoun Cup **Australia and Scotland**
14. Hillary Shield **New Zealand and England**
15. Prince William Cup **Wales and South Africa**

ANAGRAMS

1. SWAPS **WASPS**
2. ROB SLIT **BRISTOL**
3. HERN QUAILS **HARLEQUINS**
4. NIL DISHONOR **LONDON IRISH**
5. CORSET GLUE **GLOUCESTER**
6. HEFTIER EXECS **EXETER CHIEFS**
7. PHANTOMS STRONTIAN **NORTHAMPTON SAINTS**
8. ELECT REGISTRIES **LEICESTER TIGERS**
9. ACESCENT SNOWFALL **NEWCASTLE FALCONS**
10. WRITER ACROSS ROWER **WORCESTER WARRIORS**

NUMBERS AND POSITIONS

1. Loosehead prop
2. Hooker
3. Tighthead prop
4. Second row
5. Second row
6. Blindside flanker
7. Openside flanker
8. Number 8
9. Scrum-half
10. Fly-half
11. Left wing
12. Inside centre
13. Outside centre
14. Right wing
15. Full-back

TRIVIA

1. Television Match Official
2. Keith Wood
3. Nigel Owens
4. Fiji, Samoa and Tonga
5. Argentina, Australia, New Zealand and South Africa
6. Japan
7. George North
8. Jonathan Sexton
9. Warren Gatland
10. Red
11. 2012
12. Three
13. Jonah Lomu
14. Matt Dawson
15. Nelson Mandela
16. Matt Damon
17. Sébastien Chabal

RUGBY UNION (HARD)

(PAGE 176)

LINE-UPS

1. Mako Vunipola
2. Jamie George
3. Kyle Sinckler
4. Mario Itoje
5. Courtney Lawes
6. Tom Curry
7. Sam Underhill
8. Billy Vunipola
9. Ben Youngs
10. George Ford
11. Jonny May
12. Owen Farrell
13. Manu Tuilagi
14. Anthony Watson
15. Elliot Daly

ANAGRAMS

1. WONDERBRA **ROB ANDREW**
2. FALLEN ROWER **OWEN FARRELL**
3. PRICKLY HIVE **PHIL VICKERY**
4. CRAWLING ILL **WILL CARLING**
5. ALBION TUMBLE **BILL BEAUMONT**
6. JINNAH MORTONS **MARTIN JOHNSON**
7. JINNY KNOWS LION **JONNY WILKINSON**
8. ANALOGICAL DWELLER **LAWRENCE DALLAGLIO**

HIGHEST POINTS SCORERS OF ALL TIME

Rank	Name	Points	Country	International Career Span
1	**Dan Carter**	1,598	New Zealand	2003–15
2	**Jonny Wilkinson**	1,246	England	1998–2011
3	**Neil Jenkins**	1,090	Wales	1990–2003
4	**Ronan O'Gara**	1,083	Ireland	2000–2013
5	**Owen Farrell**	1,053	England	2012–
6	**Diego Dominguez**	1,010	Italy and Argentina	1991–2003, 1989
7	**Stephen Jones**	970	Wales	1998–2011
8	**Andrew Mehrtens**	967	New Zealand	1995–2004
9	**Jonny Sexton**	930	Ireland	2009–
10	**Michael Lynagh**	911	Australia	1984–1995

WORLD CUP 2019

1. Argentina
2. Australia
3. Canada
4. England
5. Fiji
6. France
7. Georgia
8. Ireland
9. Italy
10. Japan
11. Namibia
12. New Zealand
13. Russia
14. Samoa
15. Scotland
16. South Africa
17. Tonga
18. United States
19. Uruguay
20. Wales

TOP-FLIGHT TEAMS

Bath	Leeds	Newcastle	Rugby
Bristol	Leicester	Northampton	Sale
Bedford	Liverpool St Helens	Nottingham	Saracens
Coventry	London Irish	Orrell	Wasps
Exeter	London Scottish	Richmond	Waterloo
Gloucester	London Welsh	Rosslyn Park	West Hartlepool
Harlequins	Moseley	Rotherham	Worcester

INDIVIDUAL AWARDS

1. Keith Wood
2. Richie McCaw and Dan Carter
3. Clive Woodward
4. Bill Beaumont

EUROPEAN RUGBY CHAMPIONS CUP

1. 2011–2012 **Leinster** 42–14 Ulster
2. 2012–2013 **Toulon** 16–15 Clermont
3. 2013–2014 **Toulon** 23–6 Saracens
4. 2014–2015 **Toulon** 24–18 Clermont
5. 2015–2016 **Saracens** 21–9 Racing 92
6. 2016–2017 **Saracens** 28–17 Clermont
7. 2017–2018 **Leinster** 15–12 Racing 92
8. 2018–2019 **Saracens** 20–10 Leinster
9. 2019–2020 **Exeter Chiefs** 31–27 Racing 92
10. 2020–2021 **Toulouse** 22–17 La Rochelle

WORLD CUP FINALS

1. New Zealand, France
2. Australia, England
3. South Africa, New Zealand
4. Australia, France
5. England, Australia
6. South Africa, England
7. New Zealand, France
8. New Zealand, Australia
9. South Africa, England

TRIVIA

1. Fiji and Great Britain
2. New Zealand and England
3. USA
4. Australia and Namibia
5. Japan
6. Jonny Wilkinson (277); Gavin Hastings (227); Michael Lynagh (195)
7. Jonah Lomu and Bryan Habana (15)
8. 2000
9. Lloyds TSB (1999–2002); Royal Bank of Scotland (2003–2017); NatWest (2017); Guinness (2018–)
10. England
11. Barbarians

TENNIS (EASY)

(PAGE 183)

TRIVIA

1. **C:** Ace
2. **A:** Andy Murray
3. **B:** Deuce
4. **A:** All England Lawn Tennis Club
5. **C:** Umpire
6. **A:** John McEnroe
7. **B:** Switzerland
8. **A:** René Lacoste
9. **C:** Three times
10. **B:** Pimm's
11. **C:** Bunt
12. **B:** Venus and Serena
13. **A:** Judy
14. **B:** Cliff Richard
15. **A:** Centre Court

FIX THE FAULTS

1. Roger Federer
2. Rafael Nadal
3. Andre Agassi
4. Pete Sampras
5. Novak Djokovic
6. Martina Navratilova
7. Steffi Graf
8. Billie Jean King
9. Anna Kournikova
10. Maria Sharapova

TENNIS (MEDIUM)

(PAGE 185)

ANAGRAMS

1. LORD RAVE **ROD LAVER**
2. FAFF TIGERS **STEFFI GRAF**
3. CHER STRIVE **CHRIS EVERT**
4. HURRAH TEAS **ARTHUR ASHE**
5. REPEATS SPAM **PETE SAMPRAS**
6. RAINED SAGAS **ANDRE AGASSI**
7. ADARA FALLEN **RAFAEL NADAL**
8. DAY UNMARRY **ANDY MURRAY**
9. EBBS ROCKIER **BORIS BECKER**
10. DEVAN POLYANDRIST **LINDSAY DAVENPORT**
11. ANIMAL WIRELESS **SERENA WILLIAMS**
12. ALUMNI SWIVELS **VENUS WILLIAMS**
13. ARMANI INSIGHT **MARTINA HINGIS**
14. BEIJING KELLINA **BILLIE JEAN KING**
15. ALAN AVIATOR VARMINT **MARTINA NAVRATILOVA**

ONE-TIME WIMBLEDON CHAMPIONS

1. Lleyton Hewitt
2. Michael Stich
3. Richard Krajicek
4. Andre Agassi
5. Pat Cash
6. Martina Hingis
7. Jana Novotna
8. Maria Sharapova
9. Goran Ivanišević
10. Amélie Mauresmo

MOST GRAND SLAMS

1. 1= (20 singles titles): **Roger Federer**
2. 1= (20 singles titles): **Rafael Nadal**
3. 1= (20 singles titles): **Novak Djokovic**
4. 4 (14 singles titles): **Pete Sampras**
5. 5 (12 singles titles): **Roy Emerson**
6. 6= (11 singles titles): **Rod Laver**
7. 6= (11 singles titles): **Björn Borg**

TRIVIA

1. Australian Open (January); French Open (May–June); Wimbledon (June–July); US Open (August–September)
2. US Open
3. Arthur Ashe and Louis Armstrong
4. Melbourne
5. Rod Laver and Margaret Court
6. Roger Federer
7. Andre Agassi
8. Wimbledon
9. US Open (in 1973)
10. Billie Jean King
11. John Isner
12. Bob and Mike Bryan
13. Todd Woodbridge and Mark Woodforde, known as 'The Woodies'
14. Gordon Reid
15. Margaret Court (24), Serena Williams (23), Steffi Graf (22)

TENNIS (HARD)

(PAGE 188)

NUMBER ONES

Men:

1. Patrick Rafter, Lleyton Hewitt
2. Thomas Muster
3. Gustavo Kuerten
4. Marcelo Ríos
5. Ivan Lendl
6. Boris Becker
7. Andy Murray
8. Yevgeny Kafelnikov, Marat Safin
9. Novak Djokovic
10. Carlos Moyá, Juan Carlos Ferrero, Rafael Nadal
11. Stefan Edberg
12. Roger Federer
13. Jim Courier, Pete Sampras, Andre Agassi, Andy Roddick

Women:

1. Steffi Graf
2. Monica Seles
3. Arantxa Sánchez Vicario
4. Martina Hingis
5. Lindsay Davenport
6. Jennifer Capriati
7. Venus Williams
8. Serena Williams
9. Kim Clijsters
10. Justine Henin
11. Amélie Mauresmo
12. Maria Sharapova
13. Ana Ivanovic
14. Jelena Janković
15. Dinara Safina
16. Caroline Wozniacki
17. Victoria Azarenka
18. Angelique Kerber
19. Karolína Plíšková
20. Garbiñe Muguruza
21. Simona Halep
22. Naomi Osaka
23. Ashleigh Barty

BATTLING BRITS

1. Bunny Austin
2. Fred Perry
3. French Open
4. John Lloyd (who reached the Australian Open final in 1977)
5. 1977
6. Pete Sampras (1998); Pete Sampras (1999); Goran Ivanišević (2001); Lleyton Hewitt (2002)
7. 2015

RECORD BREAKERS

1. Steffi Graf, Andre Agassi, Serena Williams, Rafael Nadal
2. Steffi Graf in 1988
3. Barbora Krejčíková (who won the French Open in 2021)
4. Kim Clijsters
5. Boris Becker
6. Goran Ivanišević
7. Venus and Serena Williams
8. Althea Gibson (who won the French Championships, the precursor to the French Open) in 1956
9. Chris Evert (Chris Evert-Lloyd)
10. USA (32)

NFL

(PAGE 193)

1. Seattle Seahawks
2. San Francisco 49ers
3. Los Angeles Rams
4. Los Angeles Chargers
5. Las Vegas Raiders
6. Arizona Cardinals
7. Denver Broncos
8. Dallas Cowboys
9. Houston Texans
10. Minnesota Vikings
11. Kansas City Chiefs
12. New Orleans Saints
13. Green Bay Packers
14. Chicago Bears
15. Indianapolis Colts
16. Detroit Lions
17. Cincinnati Bengals
18. Tennessee Titans
19. Atlanta Falcons
20. Cleveland Browns
21. Buffalo Bills
22. Pittsburgh Steelers
23. Carolina Panthers
24. Jacksonville Jaguars
25. Tampa Bay Buccaneers
26. Miami Dolphins
27. New England Patriots
28. New York Giants
29. New York Jets
30. Philadelphia Eagles
31. Baltimore Ravens
32. Washington Football Team

NBA

(PAGE 194)

1. Atlanta Hawks
2. Boston Celtics
3. Brooklyn Nets
4. Charlotte Hornets
5. Chicago Bulls
6. Cleveland Cavaliers
7. Dallas Mavericks
8. Denver Nuggets
9. Detroit Pistons
10. Golden State Warriors
11. Houston Rockets
12. Indiana Pacers
13. Los Angeles Clippers
14. Los Angeles Lakers
15. Memphis Grizzlies
16. Miami Heat
17. Milwaukee Bucks
18. Minnesota Timberwolves
19. New Orleans Pelicans
20. New York Knicks
21. Oklahoma City Thunder
22. Orlando Magic
23. Philadelphia 76ers
24. Phoenix Suns
25. Portland Trail Blazers
26. Sacramento Kings
27. San Antonio Spurs
28. Toronto Raptors
29. Utah Jazz
30. Washington Wizards

MLB

(PAGE 195)

1. Los Angeles Angels
2. Houston Astros
3. Oakland Athletics
4. Toronto Blue Jays
5. Atlanta Braves
6. Milwaukee Brewers
7. St. Louis Cardinals
8. Chicago Cubs
9. Arizona Diamondbacks
10. Los Angeles Dodgers
11. San Francisco Giants
12. Cleveland Indians
13. Seattle Mariners
14. Miami Marlins
15. New York Mets
16. Washington Nationals
17. Baltimore Orioles
18. San Diego Padres
19. Philadelphia Phillies
20. Pittsburgh Pirates
21. Texas Rangers
22. Tampa Bay Rays
23. Cincinnati Reds
24. Boston Red Sox
25. Colorado Rockies
26. Kansas City Royals
27. Detroit Tigers
28. Minnesota Twins
29. Chicago White Sox
30. New York Yankees